GETTING ORGANIZED IN THE GOOGLE ERA

how to get stuff out of your head,
find it when you need it,
and get it done right

GETTING ORGANIZED IN THE GOOGLE ERA

douglas c. merrill
and james a. martin

broadway books • new york

BROADWAY BOOKS and the Broadway Books colophon are trademarks of
Random House, Inc.

Library of Congress Cataloging-in-Publication Data
Merrill, Douglas Clark, 1970–
   Getting organized in the Google era: how to get stuff out of your head,
find it when you need it, and get it done right / Douglas Merrill and
James A. Martin.
     p. cm.
   Includes bibliographical references.
   1. Organization. 2. Google. 3. Memory. I. Martin, James A.
II. Title.
   HD31.M3979 2010
   650.1—dc22   2009025578
ISBN 978-0-385-52817-7

Printed in the United States of America

Design by Ralph Fowler / rlfdesign

10 9 8 7 6 5 4 3 2 1

First Edition

CONTENTS

part three **overcoming challenges,
big and small**

PREFACE

WHAT? ANOTHER BOOK on organization? "No way," you're probably thinking. I mean, does the world really need *another* book on how to get organized?

It's okay. I thought the same thing when I first began to write this book. At the time, I was the chief information officer at Google, whose corporate mission is to "organize the world's information."[1]

So apparently there were people who thought I must have useful insights to share about the challenges of being organized in the information age.

Out of sheer politeness, I sat down with my colleague (and now most excellent coauthor) Jim Martin to talk about organization. As it turned out, I found I had plenty of new ideas to offer.

But first, please allow me a brief digression.

Picture, if you will, a small, thin young boy with a buzz cut and thick glasses. He's seated next to his mother at a long, dark wooden table. The table's too high for him, so his legs dangle from his chair as he sits up as tall as he can. It's a summer afternoon during the 1970s in Conway, Arkansas, a small, bucolic town. Outside, it's hazy-hot and stagnant;

only the mosquitoes are moving. Inside, it's cool, with the air conditioner humming in the background.

Despite the languid pace of this late summer afternoon in this quiet southern town, the boy's pulse is racing.

His mother is patiently guiding her son through the multiplication tables. It's not the first time they've done this, nor even the second. Practicing addition, subtraction, and multiplication, sometimes for hours at a time, every summer before school starts has become a routine for them.

> Second verse
> same as the first.
>
> —Herman's Hermits,
> "I'm Henry VIII, I Am"

If you knew this boy's family background, you'd have expected him to be a math wiz. His father has a doctorate in physics, and his mother holds two master's degrees. One older sister followed in her father's footsteps to earn an undergraduate degree in physics; the other has a degree in British literature of the Middle Ages. His older brother holds a doctorate in, of all things, mathematics.

And yet, here's the youngest child, struggling summer after summer to learn something as basic as multiplication. What a failure he is! He constantly worries everyone will figure out he's not smart enough or not good enough or that he's an embarrassment to his family.

As you've probably guessed by now, I am that boy. Or I was—I'm taller now, with longer hair. But I still remember how that secret fear set my heart pounding.

Though I didn't know it then, I was bad at math because I'm dyslexic. Dyslexia is a learning disorder affecting some 10 million kids in the United States alone.[2] Because dyslexia causes the brain to reverse numbers, dyslexics often have a hard time in math. Reading is difficult too because dyslexics also reverse letters.

Back then, dyslexia was far less recognized and diagnosed than it is today, and I was in high school before I realized it was the root cause of my learning difficulties. Luckily, my parents were patient with me and my siblings helped me with my homework. I worked hard, and, over time, I managed to

Preface

viii

do reasonably well in academics. Eventually I too earned a doctorate. Perhaps not so surprisingly, mine's in cognitive science—the study of how people learn and solve problems. I studied cognitive science because I wanted to figure out how to help that boy—and others like him—stop feeling so scared, sad, and anxious about learning.

In my research, I found that most of the ways we teach math (and other subjects) are poorly designed for how our brains actually work. Dyslexic or not, most of us have trouble learning math not because we're stupid or lazy but because we're simply being taught in the wrong ways. In fact, I realized that most of how our world is structured is wrong for how our brains work, which makes being organized extremely difficult. (I'll explain this further in chapter 1.)

Given all these obstacles to learning (on top of my dyslexia), how did I, that scared kid, end up earning a doctorate and becoming the CIO at Google? Well, I did spend an inordinate amount of time in punk clubs, but I don't think that's relevant here. Kidding aside, here's the deal: Because learning was such a struggle for me, I spent a lot of time thinking about how to get around the limitations my learning challenges posed. I worked hard to develop techniques and systems to reduce the stress on my brain and help me focus on only the information I really needed to learn. I couldn't take anything for granted.

These extra efforts I made, these systems I developed for organizing information, helped me eventually succeed in school. Years later, as luck would have it, my efforts paid off in my career too. I was hired to help Google "organize the world's information" partly because I'd been practicing to do that very thing, on an admittedly much smaller scale, since first grade.

Spending both my childhood and entire adult life developing systems of organization has taught me many things. Not least is the fact that many of us are disorganized today because we haven't taken into account our brain's inherent limitations. And we haven't found ways of working around those constraints. My brain's shortcomings happen to include dyslexia, but the fact is, we're all brain-constrained in some way.

Take memory, for example. Our short-term memory can hold between only five and nine things at once. With endless to-do items competing for our attention, plus the countless bits of information we gather all day, it's no wonder we're constantly forgetting things. Shifting from one task to another complicates matters too, by knocking out what we had in our short-term memories. That's one reason that our brains simply can't handle multitasking.

Sadly, our brains aren't good at making decisions either. For example, too often, we make choices based on our fear of losing something, rather than our hope of gaining something. Considering the many choices we're faced with at any given time, it's no wonder we feel mentally drained by day's end.

Our brains aren't the only reason we're disorganized and stressed. We're also held back by many of the ways in which the world is structured today. Without realizing it, we continue to organize our lives around outdated societal structures and beliefs that are totally wrong for what we need now. For example, businesses today continue to revolve around a schedule whose original purpose was to organize factory workers, even though we're largely an information and service economy today and adhering to the factory schedule creates stress and lots of other problems. We still send our children to school based on a schedule devised long ago so they could work the fields (and I don't mean baseball fields). We live by rules laid out in a time long gone. A time before life centered on computers. When only one parent worked. When knowledge was power. When the commute between home and office was usually brief—and the boundaries separating the two were distinct.

Ah, the good old days.

And yet, our current societal structures depend on our having excess brainpower so we can always remember when to drop the kids off at soccer practice or ballet class, where our keys are, and when that all-important sales presentation is due and who needs to approve it. This enormous disconnect between how we *think* our brains and societal structures work and how they *actually* work, combined with all the information vying for our attention, is at the heart of our disorganization today.

This problem is also compounded by the fact that if anything goes wrong, our stress levels go supernova on us. In fact, your stress probably compelled you to pick up this book. (Thank you for that, by the way.) Maybe it causes you to write to-do lists that never shrink. To worry how you'll find time to help your children with their studies. To feel, as I often do, that you're always behind.

Let's face it, disorganization causes stress. Stress makes you flounder. Floundering makes you even more stressed. That makes you flounder more. It's the perfect definition of a downward spiral.

I know something about that spiral. I've been caught in it before.

When Jim and I started working on this book, I was in the middle of switching jobs, changing cities, and searching for a new house. I had just left Google to become president of EMI Music's digital business and its chief operating officer of new music. (EMI is one of the top four music labels.) EMI hired me, in part, to help the company navigate the complicated technical and organizational challenges the industry has been struggling with because of consumers' shift to digital music.

> You run and you run to catch up with the sun / But it's sinking.
>
> —Pink Floyd, "Time"

As both a music and tech junkie, it was a challenge dear to my heart. But moving from Silicon Valley to Los Angeles caused me to face a lot of other challenges too. I thought I'd never learn where the grocery store in my new city was, let alone how my new company worked. I was no longer able to follow the systems and structures I'd built for myself. Suddenly, I was that boy with a buzz cut again, feeling like the only one who doesn't get it, who's struggling, who's staying up late trying to figure out how to do some task that should be easy. I was incredibly stressed. Luckily, I worked my way through the stress using the various organizational techniques I developed, and which I'll describe later in this book.

So my dyslexia gave me a vested interest in understanding how we learn. My studies in cognitive science helped me see how the brain and our societal structures work against us. With this knowledge and perspective, I came to understand the importance of identifying the root causes of disorganization. Unfortunately, that's something most books on organization gloss over or ignore. Not this one. I want this book to help you understand why you're not as organized as you'd like, because as you'll soon see, *it's not your fault.* There are forces larger than you conspiring to keep you feeling scattered.

The good news is that you're far from powerless. I'll share with you strategies for overcoming the challenges that cause you to be unproductive and stressed at work and in your personal life. I won't be talking about things like how to organize the clothes in your closet (that's something you could teach *me*). Rather, I want to share with you my techniques for organizing the tasks and information in your life so you can achieve your goals more efficiently and effectively, and with the least amount of worry.

Similarly, I'm not going to offer one-size-fits-all notions of being organized. Always keep your e-mail inbox empty? Arrange computer files into folders within folders? Get financial statements delivered electronically? If I had to go through life doing things like that, I'd forever be DOA: Disorganized on Arrival.

The truth is, even if they may *sound* like good organizational principles, I don't do any of those things. It's not because I can't. It's because I've figured out ways that are better suited to the world in which we live and work today.

For example, my years at Google helped me understand how technology can help us to organize, rather than be overwhelmed by, the information that assaults us every day. I saw how technology can help make our lives easier by helping us be more organized and efficient, and I saw how it can help reduce our stress levels by minimizing the strain on our memory and letting our brains work for, rather than against, us.

That's why I wanted to write this book: to share with you the methods I've developed (some use technology, some don't) for getting around the limitations our brains, our societal structures, and our personal constraints impose on us.

My goal is to help you develop your own system—one that works for you—for being more organized, more successful, and less stressed. I want to help you stop doing things that waste time and energy you didn't even know you were wasting. And I want to help you decide what's important to do—and what's important *not* to do. Through awareness, effort, and better organization, you'll find yourself in an *upward* spiral. Each day will bring you a bit more clarity and excess mental capacity, which you can fill with things that are a lot more fun, productive, and important than stress. That's the kind of spiral I like.

Organizing a Book About Organization

So that's this book. In Part One, I'll be talking about you. How you think. How you feel. What your society looks like

WHAT'S WITH THE LYRICS?

I've been writing for a long time, in different formats, with different goals, and for different audiences. But one thing has remained constant: For many years, I've inserted music, in one way or another, into my writing.

I have a deep love of music. Whenever possible, my life plays out against a backdrop of my favorite music. For example, as I write these words, I'm listening to Pink Floyd's "Dark Side of the Moon."

I also find that, at least for me, music reduces stress. So it seemed natural that a book about reducing stress through better organization would have its own sound track.

The lyrics tell a story of their own. But in the context of this book, some of the lyrics I've chosen to insert are simply a humorous aside relating to a point I've made or a situation I've described. Sometimes, a lyric makes or reinforces a point from the prose. At other times, the connection is the song title, the performer, or the era of the music itself.

(cont.)

Mostly, though, the lyrics underscore the emotional context of the surrounding prose—what I was feeling as I wrote the words you're reading. Regardless, the lyrics always offer a glimpse inside the crazy attic I call my brain.

Maybe the lyrics will evoke similar emotions within you too. Maybe they won't. Either way, I invite you to pause when you come to a lyric to see how it makes you feel. You might be surprised.

and how it affects you. What your constraints are and how you can move beyond them. What your authentic goals are and how you can organize to meet them.

In Part Two, I'll share with you all the tips, techniques, and strategies I've developed over the years for getting and staying organized: how to search, how to organize information, and how to keep track of all your e-mails, to-do lists, documents, and calendars. I'll also point you toward some of the amazing tools and technologies—like smart phones and cloud computing—we now have at our fingertips, and I'll help you discover ways to use them that work best for you.

In Part Three, I'll talk about how to organize around the challenges, both big and small, that we face in our twenty-first-century world. I'll help you learn to minimize distractions, and I'll explain why there's no such thing as "work-life balance." I'll show you how being organized can help you tap into the energy and brain power you'll need to handle the unexpected when it comes—because it *will* come. By the time you're done reading this book, it's my hope that you'll be ready to get a fresh start on organizing your life.

So let's begin, shall we? The weather's fine, the mosquitoes aren't biting, and I promise not to ask you to recite the multiplication tables.

part one

A PANORAMIC VIEW OF YOU

chapter 1

COCKTAIL PARTIES &
CAP'N CRUNCH

a journey inside your brain

IN THIS CHAPTER
Experiencing the Cocktail Party Effect
Albert Einstein's Phone Number
Why Multitasking Doesn't Work
Moving from Short-Term to Long-Term Memory
You Ordered Sushi, the Waiter Brought Tempura Chicken
A Story About a Story
Re-creating a Chess Game
Decisions, Decisions
Reasons to Stick with Cap'n Crunch

READY TO START EXPLORING the topic of organization? Great. So am I. But first, I want you to put down this book.

Put down the book, lift up your eyes, and look around.

What do you see? No matter how boring or uniform your surroundings, I'm sure there are a remarkable number of shapes, colors, and patterns around you right now. Okay, eyes back on the page, please.

Just now, as you looked around, your eyes scanned the area using little interior lenses (and perhaps bigger ones in the form of glasses) to cast shadows, shapes, and colors onto your retinas. Your retinas hosted several chemical processes to identify visual features and transmit them to your optic nerves. Those features traveled most of the way to your visual cortex, where they were processed so you could identify what you saw, be it walls, a floor, or clouds in the distance. It's pretty amazing when you think about everything that had to happen for you to "just see."

Now let's do a quick test. Make a list of all the objects you remember seeing when you looked around. Don't cheat. Go ahead. I'll wait.

You were able to recall two, three, or four objects, right? You probably didn't remember many more than that, especially because you just read that paragraph about vision. In fact, that paragraph was a trick to distract you and make it less likely you'd remember what you saw. If I hadn't distracted you, you'd probably have recalled a few more objects. Regardless, in a day or so, it's likely you won't be able to remember any of them at all—unless you repeated them over and over in your head. (Though practice may not make perfect, it does improve memory.)

The point of this exercise was to give you a small glimpse into how our brains work. Why should you care? Because, believe it or not, the way our brains work is one of the biggest challenges we face in becoming organized.

When I was studying for my Ph.D. in cognitive science, I was constantly surprised by the amazing things the brain can do. For example, you can identify gender and estimate age just by looking at a photograph of someone's nose. You can recognize a song within a few notes. You can approximate where a Frisbee will land after only a second or so of watching its flight. You and your brain are astounding.

Yet I was equally fascinated by what the brain *doesn't* do well. The brain is especially inept at memorizing bits of information, like the objects you've just seen in a room. To some degree, this is a blessing. If we didn't forget things, we'd have all this extraneous data in our brains, which would make it more difficult to recall the important stuff.

The brain is also pretty bad at accurately remembering

events, which gets in the way of logical decision making. I know, you think you're a master decision maker. But you aren't. You think that events you remember clearly, such as plane crashes you read about in the news, are far more common than they actually are. So you decide to avoid planes because you're more afraid of airplane turbulence than you are of driving, even though you're probably in more danger driving than you are flying. I'll go into more detail about decision making later in this chapter.

Your brain also has a tendency to combine memories. The events you "recall" may have actually happened at different times with different people, but your brain has stitched them together into something else. This is why your brain may think it remembers something it can't possibly recall. For example, you might think you remember something that happened to you at age four, but in reality, you don't. It's more likely your parents told a story about you when you were at that age so often that your brain decided it remembered it. But it didn't because the brain can rarely, if ever, form lasting memories at that young an age.

Alas, in some respects, your brain may not be as amazing as you thought. But don't take it personally. Your brain was developed eons ago primarily to prevent you from being eaten by carnivorous beasts—not to memorize lists or store facts. Think about it: Your brain weighs only about three pounds.[1] You've cooked turkeys far bigger than that.

> **My brain's dead weight / I'm trying to get my head straight.**
>
> —Eminem,
> "My Name Is"

By the way, if any of you are hoping for a diagram of a brain with an arrow pointing to "the place where you organize your life," I won't be delivering it. I couldn't even if I wanted to because there are many different mental processes that play a role in how we organize information—or don't.

However, I can help you understand how your brain functions, so you can recognize all the ways it works against you and work around them. Believe it or not, that understanding can be crucial as you try to organize all the information in your life.

Fact is, we need information to do just about every-thing. The information we use on a day-to-day basis, in our jobs and our personal lives, often comes from memory. For example, just performing a simple task, such as writing an e-mail, requires us to move information stored in long-term memory, such as the facts or opinions we're expressing in the e-mail, into short-term memory. Without that process, how would we know what to write?

But we face a challenge: How do we retain all the bits and pieces that enter our brains as our attention wanders from one thing to another? Judging from the results of the memory test we performed a few pages back, we can't. Our brain is doing too many things at once. But we can learn strategies for processing and storing information that require the least amount of brain power possible. Which brings me to my first principle of organization: *Organize your life to minimize brain strain.* I'll offer suggestions for doing this throughout the book.

> **Organize your life to minimize brain strain.**

By the way, did you notice I called it a "principle" of orga-nization, rather than a "rule"? Honestly, I'm not here to give you rules. Rules are meant to restrict you. My principles are simply meant to suggest new ideas, options, and tools, so you can design systems for organizing that work for *you.*

Experiencing the Cocktail Party Effect

Before we can tackle how to minimize the brain strain caused by all the massive amounts of information clamoring for our attention every day, it helps to understand how our attention works.

Attention is a survival mechanism. Without it, we'd drown in the raging floodwaters of sensation and information. Your attention is finely honed around each of your senses. For example, you'd probably notice, as I just did, when you stubbed your toe on your desk. Or your attention might be immediately drawn to the sound of a car accident outside your window; that just happened to me too.

It makes sense that loud noises and sharp sensations would capture our attention and force themselves into our consciousness. Our senses are constantly on alert, even if we don't realize it. If nothing else, they're part of our survival mechanism, with which we're hardwired to make sure we'll be keenly aware when there's a tiger hiding in the bushes ready to pounce on us. But oddly enough, our attention can often be drawn to much subtler signals. Have you been in the middle of a loud cocktail party when over all the noise, you suddenly heard someone say your name—even though you hadn't heard a word of the speaker's conversation before she spoke your name? This is called the *cocktail party effect*, a term coined back in 1953[2] that has nothing to do, in this context at least, with hangovers.

The cocktail party effect puts a label on one of the most amazing truths about attention: At any given moment, your brain registers a lot more than you're actually aware of. Just because your brain notices something doesn't mean you're consciously aware of it, however. In this instant, your brain registers the information (your name) as relevant, so it enters your conscious attention, and your ears perk up ("he called me a *what*?").

For example, at this exact moment, what's the feeling of your right big toe? I'll wager you weren't aware of any feeling there. But now that I've mentioned it, you can, perhaps, feel a sock around it or pressure on it. Because I mentioned it, you sent a signal to your brain that it's relevant, and so you've focused your attention on it and are now experiencing its sensations. Don't worry, your focus will likely move on and you will forget your toe again (until your next pedicure).

Point is, even with all the information that washes across us constantly, the only information we really need to pay attention to is the information that we have to do something with or that matters to us in some way. The rest is just background cocktail party chatter. So how do our brains determine what information is worth holding on to and what isn't? That's where memory comes in.

After we notice something, it goes into short-term memory. Once it's there, we can decide if it means anything to us and if we need to do something with it. The purpose of short-term memory is to hold stuff for just a few seconds or minutes (hence its name). Normally, information received into short-term memory is discarded. You don't care about most things you happen to notice, like the feeling of a sock on your big toe.

> If I wait for just a second more / I know I'll forget what I came here for.
>
> —Yaz, "Nobody's Diary"

Often, however, you want to remember something longer than a few minutes—like a phone number or a person's name. There's a problem, however. Our short-term memories can hang on to only between five and nine things, max, at one time. If you try to store ten things in short-term memory, it will drop something—just as you do when you try to carry three bulging grocery bags up a flight of stairs. You'll forget one or more bits you're currently carrying around.

> **Get stuff out of your head as quickly as possible.**

The inability to hold on to more than nine scraps of information in short-term memory brings me to my second principle of organization, one that many books about organization advocate: *Get stuff out of your head as quickly as possible*. If you don't, you're likely to overload your short-term memory and forget what you wanted to remember.

Why Multitasking Doesn't Work

Most of the time, our attention is focused on one thing. And at this exact moment, you may have chuckled because you were cooking dinner, watching the news on TV, rid-

A reporter was out for a walk with Albert Einstein and asked for Einstein's phone number, in case there were any follow-up questions. Einstein readily agreed to give it, walked over to a pay phone, picked up the phone book, looked up his number, and read it to the reporter. In response to the reporter's astonishment, Einstein said something like, "Why remember my number, when it's in the phone book?"

Yes, I doubt the story's true too. But it's funny. And it illustrates the need to get stuff out of your head, so you can focus on what's important.

ing a stationary bicycle, and reading that sentence all at the same time.

Multitasking is something we all do these days. The problem is, our brains just aren't cut out for it. When you multitask, you're interfering with your brain's efforts to put information into short-term memory—a process that's fragile enough to begin with. And if the information doesn't make it into short-term memory, you won't be able to recall it later.

That's why multitasking often works against us. Yes, you can walk and chew gum at the same time. You can fold laundry while talking to a friend on the phone. Clowns can ride a unicycle while juggling brightly colored balls. These are rote tasks that don't demand a lot of brain power. But in many cases, multitasking—especially when you're trying to accomplish two dissimilar tasks, each requiring some level of thought and attention—makes it difficult to encode information into long-term memory. And that brings me to my third principle of organization: *Multitasking usually makes you less efficient.*

Multitasking usually makes you less efficient.

For example, at Google, there was a commonly accepted practice of having laptops open during meetings. It wasn't that people didn't care about the meetings. It's just that folks had lots of different things to do, and juggling several at once seemed efficient. It wasn't. Eventually, it became obvious that many of us were missing lots of important stuff that came out of meetings because we were multitasking and weren't fully paying attention to what was going on around us. We either didn't hear what was said, or we heard it but didn't focus our attention on it, which meant it had no hopes of making it into short-term memory.

When it became clear that having laptops open in meetings was actually lowering productivity, some Google meetings were declared "laptop free." This, of course, generated an unintended consequence. When people thought they had something more important to do, they simply got up and left the meeting. This was a bit distracting for presenters, but at least it was a more effective use of the escapees' attention. (Used the right ways, laptops can actually bring people together in a meeting, instead of causing them to focus on things that have nothing to do with the meeting. You'll see what I mean in chapter 11.)

> **You just turn your pretty head and walk away.**
>
> —James Gang,
> "Walk Away"

Multitasking can be expensive too. I learned that lesson not long ago by sending a text message while driving (multitasking on the road is an especially bad idea, by the way). I was pulling up to a stoplight, and unfortunately, I misjudged the distance between my car and the one in front because I wasn't fully paying attention. Naturally, I hit the other car. Nobody was hurt, but it was the most expensive text message I've ever sent. (Don't worry, I no longer text while driving, and, in fact, it's now illegal in California and other states.)

Moving from Short-Term to Long-Term Memory

Let's assume that each time you receive a new bit of information, you're paying attention and you aren't multitasking.

How do you hold on to that piece of information beyond a few minutes? You move it from short-term memory into long-term memory using a process cognitive scientists call *encoding*.

The term *encoding* implies that something is being converted from one format into another. In terms of the brain, information held in short-term memory takes a different form when it enters long-term memory. You can see this for yourself using a phone number example.

Kindly tap into your long-term memory to recall a time when a would-be sweetheart first gave you his or her phone number. If you didn't have anything to write with at the time, you probably tried to memorize it. How?

You may have repeated the number over in your head, digit by digit, several times. Cognitive scientists call this process *rehearsal*. By rehearsing the number, you encoded it from short-term to long-term memory. And that encoding allowed you to call your future honey later, as promised. (Okay, so a lot of people today don't even remember their spouse's cell phone number because it's stored in their own cell phone's memory. But work with me here.)

> Rikki don't lose
> that number…
> Send it off in a
> letter to yourself.
>
> —Steely Dan, "Rikki
> Don't Lose That
> Number"

If everything worked out and you ended up with this person for a while, you didn't have to continue rehearsing the number because it was now stored in long-term memory. However, once you learned the number, you might have noticed something odd. You could remember the entire number, no problem, but you couldn't easily recall some of the individual digits out of sequence. For example, if I asked you for the fifth digit of your honey's phone number, you wouldn't be able to recall it without some effort. You'd likely need to start at the beginning and then mentally walk through the digits, one by one, until you arrived at the fifth.

Notice the difference in how you recalled the number when you were first encoding it and how you recalled it later. When you were rehearsing the number, it was a bunch of individual digits. Once encoded, the number became a single thing, no longer made up of individual units.

Yes, but who cares? Granted, it's unlikely you'll ever need to identify the fifth digit of a phone number from memory. But this example illustrates a difficulty we face in remembering things: Our brains have trouble retrieving information in a form or context that differs from the one in which the information was originally encoded. As we'll soon see, this difficulty can be a huge obstacle to being organized.

The point to encode here is that it's hard to move information into long-term memory in a way that makes it easy to recall that data when you need it later. If you can't recall the information, you can't use it, which means it's just taking up space, like that pair of old rain boots in the back of your closet. But this is the key point about encoding: If you're distracted, you'll fail to encode the information at all. This means you'll have zero chance of recalling that information later. In other words, you've wasted your time.

Short of repeating the information over and over in your head (not the most efficient method—plus you run the risk of accidentally doing it aloud, which just makes you look silly), how do you increase the chances of successfully transferring information into long-term memory so you can easily recall it later? By associating a story with it.

You Ordered Sushi, the Waiter Brought Tempura Chicken

I know: You think you have a great memory. I believe you. But I'll bet you still struggle, at least occasionally, to call up arbitrary pieces of information. For example, do you still recall all the objects I asked you to try to remember a few pages ago? You have a slightly better chance of remembering a few objects this time around because we rehearsed this a minute ago. But I'm betting you can't come up with all of them.

However, if I had given you a list of objects and asked you to pick out the ones you remember seeing, it's likely you would do even better. That's because this task involves recognition, not recall. Because of how your brain encodes and retrieves data, recognition is a much easier task. That's why you want to take a multiple-choice test if you get the chance.

Unfortunately, most of our lives are organized around recall, and we don't get many multiple-choice tests in real life.

Let's pause again for another quick memory test. When was the last time you ordered something in a restaurant, but when the food arrived, it was the wrong dish? To answer my question, you're probably thinking, "Hmmm, where might I have ordered food, but gotten something else? Maybe someplace where they didn't speak my language well? Oh, right, there was that night at the Japanese restaurant...."

Most likely, your recollection of an instance of being served the wrong food was in the form of a *story*. Your brain found a story—a memory of a prior experience—in which you were given the wrong food. It didn't just retrieve a fact about this experience out of some dusty filing cabinet in your brain; it retrieved the people, places, and things related to the fact. And from that story you may be able to recall certain other facts, such as what you ordered, what you were served, maybe the name of the restaurant, or even what you were wearing (especially if the waiter accidentally decorated your shirt with teriyaki sauce).

The word *story* is key. We tend to remember facts not as facts per se but as elements of a story. Facts are dry and usually boring. We can't relate to facts, so our minds don't absorb them easily. Stories are another matter. Stories have everything that facts lack: color, action, characters, sights, smells, sounds, and emotions, all of which we can relate to. We can picture ourselves doing, not doing, or having already done what the story describes. Stories put facts into a meaningful, and therefore memorable, context.

By definition, being organized requires having bits of information stored in a useful order. Putting these bits into order requires encoding them and recalling them correctly. Your brain wants to recall information not as bits and chunks, but as stories. Thus, finding ways to embed facts into stories is essential to becoming better organized.

To recall a fact, it helps to try and remember what you were doing when your mind first noted that fact—in other words, to recall a story that gives the fact context. What you were doing is the story the fact relates to. I see this in action often, when my wife, Sonya, is trying to locate her purse. She wanders around the house mumbling to herself: "Now, I remember I was in here, watching the dogs, and then I went over there to pick up the magazine and...Ah! I took my lipstick out in the bathroom!" She's recounting a story that explains how her purse might have been lost and what she was doing at the time she last held it in her hand. The story is what helps her remember where she put the purse she (regularly) misplaces. Of course, she could always put her purse in the same place and then just recall that place. But that's not her style.

The strategy of always doing something the same way in order to remember it works for finding one's purse. But it doesn't work for most other things we make and things we do. This is where stories can help. And that brings us to my fourth principle of organization: *Use stories to remember.*

Use stories to remember.

During my first months at EMI, I did a lot of media interviews about the issues the company faced, particularly relating to digital music rights. For the press interviews and speeches I gave, I needed some facts at my disposal, such as the percentage of album sales generated by the top 200 selling albums.

Facts, when sprinkled judiciously throughout a talk, strengthen your argument and illustrate your themes and points. However, I'm quite bad at recalling facts and particularly poor at remembering numerical ones. And I couldn't exactly say to reporters, "Hey, hold on a sec while I look up something online, so I can explain what I mean." Instead, I used a better strategy of weaving the facts I wanted to remember into a story about music fans and their needs. It was a story about how the world is changing, how those changes are playing out through our purchasing behaviors, and how those behaviors relate to the percentage of album sales for the top two hundred albums.

I didn't try to remember the percentage by itself. I just

focused on remembering that story. The percentage came along for the ride, like a fly on the fruit I pick in my backyard. The story gave that particular shard of information meaning, which made it easier for me to recall and, I hope, for others to see the points I was trying to make.

Let me put principle no. 4 another way: To use stories for recall, it helps to think about what you'll later want to do with that bit of data *before* you encode it. Then you can embed the information in a story in a way that will make it easier to recall later. This isn't simple, of course. You aren't the Amazing Kreskin, so you probably can't predict the future. However, if you can figure out why or how you might need to remember a piece of information, you can do a better job of encoding it.

> Everybody in the whole cell block / Was dancin' to the jailhouse rock.
>
> —Elvis Presley, "Jailhouse Rock"

Later on, I'll share a technique for doing this—using stories—that doesn't require you to see into the future.

A STORY ABOUT A STORY

If you think about it, you can associate a story with just about anything. Even *Waiting for Godot*—a play first produced in 1953 and famous for its lack of story—has a story. It's about two bums sitting around waiting for someone who never shows.

In fact, there's even a story behind the story of *Waiting for Godot*. As it turns out, the play was often produced in prisons.[3] The theme of waiting in vain apparently resonated with inmates, and the playwright, Samuel Beckett, struck up friendships with some of his incarcerated audience members. Beckett even gave one former San Quentin prisoner financial support for years. So if you're trying to encode the plot and themes of *Waiting for Godot* for a test, the story about the prison inmates will make your task a little easier.

Re-creating a Chess Game

Cognitive scientists studying what is called the *novice-expert shift* (how people get from being novices to experts at something) have shown an interesting demonstration of how stories give information context, which, in turn, helps us remember that information.

In one well-known set of studies, researchers took a chess board, played a set of moves so it appeared the game was halfway completed, then covered the board. One by one, researchers brought in people who didn't play chess and showed them the board for a few minutes. After exiting, the novices were asked to re-create the positions of the pieces on a different chess board. They couldn't do it.

Next, researchers brought in chess experts and asked them to do the same task. The experts fared much better at re-creating the board.

Then, the researchers performed the same task again. But this time, they arranged the pieces on the board randomly. There was no way a real game could have caused the pieces to be positioned on the board in that way. In this version of the study, researchers saw no difference between novices and experts in re-creating the board.

The experts fared better in the first study because they recognized the context of the game that yielded the organization of the pieces. When they looked at the board, they didn't see a collection of rooks, pawns, and knights. Rather, they saw a story of moves and countermoves that put the pieces where they were on the board. As seasoned chess players, they'd experienced that story before. "Retelling" the story enabled them to re-create the board.

But when the pieces were randomly positioned, the experts had no context or story to recount. They had to fall back on usual, fallible strategies for remembering. Since the experts were using the same strategies as the novices, with no stories to help them, it's not surprising they did no better than the novices.

Decisions, Decisions

So our brains aren't good at remembering. They're not particularly hot at multitasking either. But there was something else I was going to mention while I was on the subject. What was it? Oh, yes. *Decisions*. Our brains are lousy at those too.

There are lots of reasons why our brains are bad at making decisions. One reason is what's known as *option confusion*. Another name for it could be "Wow, the menu at this restaurant is too long and overwhelming so I'll just have the usual thankyouverymuch." Often, when we're faced with too many choices, we'll opt for whatever is most familiar (which is probably why you've never tasted three quarters of the menu at your favorite restaurant). But what about when we're presented with new choices? Sometimes we keep changing our minds.

Imagine you're a student with an exam tomorrow. Being sensible, you and some classmates head to the library to study. On the way, you see a flyer for a local rock band, appearing that night at a nearby café. Some members of your group continue on to the library. Others decide to head for the café. That's cool; sometimes music is as important as studying.

The group en route to the café encounters yet another flyer. This one advertises a reading that night by a popular author at a local bookstore. Some group members decide to skip the café and go to the reading. Others continue on to the café. But a few—and this is where it gets interesting—decide to backtrack and head to the library after all.

Some famous cognitive scientists have studied this phenomenon. They concluded that, when presented with a new choice, we tend to question or revisit a decision we've already made. Sometimes this is rational. You might receive new information that strongly suggests that an earlier decision was incorrect. Or circumstances may have changed since you made a decision.

Usually, though, when we change a decision just because we've got a new choice, it's because our brains feel taxed by all the options. In the study, the reading versus music versus library choices wore some students down until they simply reverted back to an earlier decision.

So how can you help your brain make a decision based on the actual desirability of the outcome instead of based on habit or cognitive bias? My wife, Sonya, has a strategy. She tries various choices on for size by visualizing the end results in her mind. She'll *seem* to make a decision and keep reviewing it until she has visualized all the potential outcomes. Then she'll go around the loop again, with the new option. What she's really doing is "living" with a decision temporarily, to see how it feels and what its possible ramifications might be. By doing this, Sonya can choose the decision that ultimately feels right to her. Maybe you do this too. By looking at each option, one by one, you can avoid overtaxing your brain with too many choices at once. You're more likely to hone in on the choices that will achieve the most desirable results too.

By the way, I think it's important to surround yourself with people who have different decision-making styles, along with diverse knowledge, skill sets, and life experiences. Diversity makes it more likely that you and your colleagues will excel at your goals.

Reasons to Stick with Cap'n Crunch

Clearly, too many choices, whether big or small, quickly overwhelm our brains. For example, the next time you're in a large U.S. supermarket, take a stroll down the cereal aisle. Imagine that you're simply trying to choose a new cereal that might appeal to your taste buds or meet your dietary restrictions (or, ideally, both). My guess is that your brain will quickly become overwhelmed by the wall of brightly colored boxes. You'll probably end up feeling stressed and saying, "The heck with it, I'll stick with Cap'n Crunch." (Even then, you'll have to decide which flavor you want. But I digress.)

Ultimately, the key to making decisions is to understand what your goals are and prioritize them. In this example, if your priority is taste, you can probably rule out those ultra-healthy, fiber-rich cereals (which in my opinion taste like strands of rope). If your priority is nutrition, you may want to (with a pang of regret) forego the Cap'n Crunch. Point is, your goals will help you filter out what factors are unimportant, which in turn makes it easier to reach a decision. In this book I'll be talking a lot about the importance of goals because goals help you stay focused on what's important, which helps you be better organized.

As you can see, our brains are magnificent, but their limitations are huge. That's why it's so important to develop organizational systems to compensate for the limitations of our brains.

Ideally, our organizational systems should take into account our other constraints too, such as the social, occupational, and educational structures that work against us. They should also factor in our goals and available resources. The organizational methods we develop for ourselves should challenge our assumptions about what we do and why we do it; emphasize the importance of filtering out what's not important and focus on what is; and take advantage of the best tools—whether they are paper or digital—for each job given the rapidly changing demands, and possibilities, of today's world. For example, I'd argue that a lot of information we've traditionally tried to store in our brains can be outsourced to the Internet. You'll learn more about all of the above beginning with the next chapter.

In the meantime, do you remember in what year *Waiting for Godot* premiered? Oh well, don't worry. You can always look it up.

ENCODE THIS

- Our brain is one of the biggest challenges we face in becoming organized. It is inept at memorizing bits of information, multitasking, and making decisions. But there are ways to get around our brain's limitations.

- Because our brain often works against us, it helps to understand how it functions. That understanding can guide us as we try to improve our organization skills, and it can help us devise systems that let our brains work for, rather than against, us.

- At any given moment, your brain registers a lot more than you're actually aware of. Generally, only the information that's relevant to us makes it into our consciousness.

- After we notice something, it goes into short-term memory. Once it's there, we can decide if it means anything and if we need to do something with it.

- To remember something, you have to move it from short-term to long-term memory. That's called *encoding*.

- The best way to encode something is to associate a story with it. Stories are much easier to remember than facts.

- To use stories for recall, think about what you want to do with that bit of data before you encode it.

- Avoid wasting brain energy by being selective about what you try to remember.

chapter 2

SUMMER VACATIONS, SUBURBIA & FACTORY SHIFTS

overcoming organizational challenges in a disorganized world

SO YOUR BRAIN'S OFTEN working against you, keeping you from remembering information you need to be organized. But that's not the end of the story. There are external forces working against you too. I'm just going to come right out and say it: From an organizational standpoint, everything in our world is wrong. The way in which our work structures are organized is wrong. Our educational, societal, and community structures are wrong. Some of our most widely held assumptions about business? You guessed it: Wrong.

The end result is that, every day, you're doing things wrong. You probably don't even realize it because you've been doing things wrong your entire life. By the way, it's not your fault. You don't need fixing. It's our world and how we react to it that needs adjusting.

With everything in our world truly, madly, deeply wrong, it's no wonder our stress levels are stratospheric. There's never enough time to do everything we're convinced we must do. We feel left-handed in a right-handed world. We live on the edge and give ourselves no space to step back from the cliff. At best, we feel disorganized. At worst, defeated.

> **We're living in a powder keg and giving off sparks.**
> —Bonnie Tyler, "Total Eclipse of the Heart"

Let me give you an example. When your alarm clock goes off, it's like the start of a horse race. School begins at 8:30. You have to get the kids ready and drop them off so you can be at work by 9. Everyone rushes around the house in a tizzy. You're trying to jet off some quick e-mails and check your calendar for the day's appointments. You've also got to make sure the kids are dressed, their lunch boxes are packed, and they have their homework. Finally, everyone jumps into the car with their various jackets and lunches and backpacks and briefcases. You peel out of the driveway, merge onto the freeway—and promptly become lodged in traffic because everyone else is trying to drop off their kids at school before work too. This scene, played out every weekday all over the world, is amazingly suboptimal for the players and for society.

Here's another example. Every day, you arrive at work with a triple latte and a long list of must-dos. You sit at your desk, turn on your computer, and begin reading the dozens of e-mails that arrived overnight. You get called into an impromptu conference, then your cell phone rings. Before you know it, it's lunchtime, and you've accomplished nada on your must-do list.

Okay, one more. Later that night, you're reheating leftovers (with the day you've had, who has time and energy to prepare a meal?). Your 1980s-era combination oven-microwave finally expires. The next day, you go to the store and buy a new oven. The store ships the oven to your home, where it now sits, awaiting the professional service you've hired to install it. In a rare free moment during your workday, you call the installation service to schedule an appointment, but you get the company's answering machine. Eventually, someone from the service calls back, on your home phone. Unfortunately, it's three o'clock on a Wednesday, and you're at the office. By the time you return home and hear the message, the installation service office is closed. This painful *Groundhog Day* grind continues for days. Meanwhile, your kitchen is populated with two ovens, neither of which works. And you feel like someone's strumming your last good nerve like a banjo at a bluegrass festival.

These three stories may seem disconnected. But in reality, they're just three among countless examples of how the nine-to-five workday, one of the most deeply ingrained structures in our society, is wrong, in ways large and small.

Our work structures weren't always so wrong for what we need. They just evolved that way because we haven't significantly adapted our societal, cultural, and work structures for the realities of today's world. Our structures aren't organized in ways that actually make sense for our needs today, so our brains get overtaxed. We have very little excess mental capacity to deal with the unexpected. We flounder, we get stressed, we flounder some more.

> Another working day has ended / Only the rush hour hell to face.
>
> —The Police, "Synchronicity II"

Nine to Five: What a Way to Make a Living

How did we end up like this? Let's start by taking a look at how the nine-to-five workday, Monday–Friday workweek evolved: from the Industrial Revolution.

The revolution began in the late 1700s in the United Kingdom.[1] During the 1800s, it spread to Belgium, France (no stranger to revolutions), Germany, the United States, and other prosperous countries. The impact was enormous. It created new industries, new things to buy; new social classes, new cities and villages; new ways to travel and communicate.

In the early decades of the Industrial Revolution, people often worked from ten to sixteen hours a day.[2] Night shifts were common. At the time, this was seen as smart business—getting the most labor and output out of every twenty-four-hour period. Then, in 1881, along came a twenty-five-year-old named Frederick Winslow Taylor.[3] An employee of Midvale Steel Works, Taylor performed the first scientific management study. With a wristwatch and a notepad, he analyzed the time and efforts that factory workers spent on their tasks. After timing and writing everything down, he divided the workers' tasks into their smallest movements. Taylor believed with this approach, factories could minimize movement and effort, create more productive divisions of labor, and improve economies of scale. Taylor concluded that eliminating as many variations as possible in factory work would increase productivity too.

> Keep on working / till you're fit to drop.
> —Fine Young Cannibals, "I'm Not Satisfied"

Taylor's theories were revolutionary. Efficiency became a new religion in the business world, and Taylor its high priest. There was a drive to achieve sameness in all types of corporations because variation was seen as the enemy of efficiency. Scientific management, known as Taylorism after its founder, spread throughout the industrialized world.[4]

Eventually, manufacturers under the influence of Taylorism built the first moving assembly lines. The manufacturing parts now moved past the workers, not vice versa. Factories began to realize enormous productivity gains. By 1914, the Ford Motor Company had developed assembly lines capable of building a Model T chassis in 93 minutes, compared to the 728 minutes it once took.[5]

In order for an assembly line to work, all the workers had to be there at the same time. After all, if the worker in charge of putting the spark plug in the engine comes into work at noon, none of the cars made that morning will start. So businesses made all workers show up at a certain place at a certain time with little to no variation. And after a set of labor movements that called for a workday of no longer than eight hours, we settled on a forty-hour workweek.

Voilà! The nine-to-five workday was born. And at the time it made perfect sense. Output grew, efficiency increased, and companies profited, just as Taylor had envisioned.

Over time, nine to five (or eight to five with an hour lunch break) was adopted by many nonindustrial businesses too. Taylorism even impacted education. Since most students would end up working on assembly lines, or so the thinking went, schools should train kids to be ready for them. The idea was to give students standardized start and end times, clear homework deliverables, and the same books and tasks. It was an assembly line approach to education, with the unfortunate result of taking creative children and turning them into duplicate drones.

Okay, let's recap: The Industrial Revolution led to Taylorism, which led to assembly lines, which led to nine-to-five workdays and forty-hour workweeks. The forty-hour workweek is still our primary organization for work, even though most of us no longer work in factories and new technologies let us work when and where we want. This is true even though our reliance on standardized workweeks of forty hours has led to endless traffic gridlock, child care constraints, and loads of stress on our everyday lives. So why do we keep dancing to the same old nine-to-five song, even though our feet are killing us?

"To have meetings," you might reply. And that's true, to some degree. We need some consistent, overlapping hours so we can get together, plan, problem-solve, bond, and, inevitably, conspire against our bosses. People working together also give a company its distinctive culture, which can by itself be a reason to work there, as is the case with companies like Google and Apple.

Another argument: Though customer service (at least in terms of telephone support) is often outsourced to countries far away, businesses still need to operate their corporate functions within standard hours to be available to their suppliers and clients and customers.

So who was this dude who taught us everything we know about organization and efficiency?

Frederick Winslow Taylor was born in Philadelphia in 1856, the son of a lawyer and an abolitionist.[6] A smart kid, Taylor was accepted at Harvard Law. But too much studying at night caused his eyesight to fail, so he left school. By 1875,[7] his vision restored, Taylor became an apprentice patternmaker for a pump manufacturing company. Three years later, he went to work for Midvale Steel Works, where he was regularly promoted.

While at Midvale, Taylor performed in 1881 what was believed to be the first scientific management study—a close observation of how factory workers performed their tasks. The results of his studies became the foundations of the guiding principles he developed and promoted for businesses, schools, and just about every other type of organization in existence.

Taylor believed managers should do all the thinking and workers should stick to working—because they weren't capable of thinking anyway. As you might imagine, he wasn't terribly beloved by workers and unions. Here's Taylor, speaking at a congressional hearing:

"I can say, without the slightest hesitation, that the science of handling pig-iron is so great that the man who is... physically able to handle pig-iron and is sufficiently phlegmatic and stupid to choose this for his occupation is rarely able to comprehend the science."[8]

After leaving Midvale, Taylor became the general manager of the Manufacturing Investment Company (1890–1893) and later, one of the first management consultants. By the time of his death in 1915, Taylor had received over forty patents and authored several successful publications, including *The Principles of Scientific Management* (1911). The book's still in print. You can even download it to an Amazon Kindle.[9] How efficient is that?

Management and human resources departments need to measure job performance too. How can they do that if everyone's working at different times? And don't many people—including yours truly—simply need a formal work structure to keep them focused? To the first question I'd answer that job performance could just as easily be measured, for most jobs anyway, by the quality and quantity of output—factors that are independent of the actual hours within the workday that an employee works. As for the second question, I know plenty of people who are more focused and productive when allowed to work their own hours, either from the office or from home.

There are other reasons businesses stick to the nine-to-five workday, like the fact many bosses don't trust workers. They want everyone at the office at the same time, so they can be assured that no one's goofing off. That's something I've never understood. Why would you hire someone you don't trust?

Ultimately, however, I think we stick with the nine-to-five workday because it's so deeply engrained in our culture. It's a perfect example of how we tend to *satisfice*—make decisions and changes that are not ideal but are just good enough—rather than try to make radical changes. (*Satisfice* is a blend of the words *satisfy* and *suffice*.) The thought of tossing out the nine-to-five workday for a newer, more flexible model is overwhelming, even revolutionary. It seems much easier to force-fit our lives into the nine-to-five constraints we know and don't love than it is to change because the change process itself will cause us stress and tax our brains.

There have been efforts to break away from the nine-to-five workday schedule, of course. Broadband Internet access and cheap communication and computer costs have made working from home possible. But all too often, teleworkers still operate within the nine-to-five constraints. They're just doing it at home in workout clothes, with breaks for dog walking and *Dr. Phil*.

The globalization of world economies has also begun to chip away at the nine-to-five rock. Most of the time, however, globalization just has us working longer hours because we're still working nine to five and, in addition, being on call to deal with companies in other time zones who still follow the nine-to-five structure.

I don't have a brilliant solution to this problem, by the way. I don't have the answers to global warming or world hunger either. There are a lot of obstacles we as a society have to overcome before we can ever hope to free ourselves from the nine-to-five structure completely. But, while none of us can single-handedly change how the world is run, when it comes to our own lives, we often have a lot more control than we realize. In other words, if you find yourself stuck in the nine-to-five trap, there are things you can do about it: Talk to your boss or to the powers that be about the possibility of switching your hours or enabling you to work from home once or twice a week. Ask them to consider teleconferencing, videoconferencing, or teleworking options.

My goal is not to tell you what hours you should be working. Rather, I want to encourage you to take a look at whether your work hours are structured in a way that works for you and if not, to do something about it. To that end, allow me to introduce my fifth principle of organization: *Just because something's always been done a certain way doesn't mean it* should *be.*

> **Just because something's always been done a certain way doesn't mean it *should* be.**

Translation: Following the nine-to-five workday structure just because it's what we're used to isn't a good enough reason. In fact, it's a pretty bad one. A far smarter strategy would be one that reduced traffic, made child care simpler, and increased your ability to be productive. And unfortunately, these goals are hard to achieve within a globally preset schedule. Here's another example of why.

Do Your Kids Need Time Off to Pick Corn?

I'll bet most people reading a book about being organized in the twenty-first century don't have kids who need time off to work in the fields. But that's what most school systems in the United States give students every year. It's called *summer vacation*, and it's another example of a structure that's wrong for our world today.

Before the Industrial Revolution, economies were largely agrarian. It made sense that schools in farming communities in the United States adjourned in the spring, so kids could help their parents plant crops. Schools let out again from late summer into fall[10] so students could help with the harvests. Gradually, those breaks merged into one long summer recess. The tradition continues, even though technological advances have shifted our economy from farming to factories to service and information industries.

So what? Kids need a break from school, right? They need time off to be kids and to avoid becoming (in the words of Pink Floyd) just another brick in the wall. You want them off during the summer too so the whole family can go to Disney World. And teens need summer jobs so they can save for college, develop marketable skills, and learn to take on responsibilities.

I hear your arguments. They're perfectly good ones too. But as ideal as summer break sounds, it can actually cause stress and zap productivity for kids *and* parents. This is caused by the same problem underpinning a nine-to-five workday: During the summer break months, everyone is on vacation at the same time. Think of all those long traffic jams, full of families heading to the Hamptons or the Cape every summer weekend. Sounds unfair—how dare you add stress to my vacation? But it's real.

Plus, summer breaks force working parents to scramble for day care and/or try to find constructive things for their kids to do during the day. During the summer, parents may also feel pressure to leave work early or take more time off, in order to be with their kids. That extra time away probably makes the hours at work even more stressful because they've got the same amount of work to do in less time.

Then there's the financial hit. Parents who take extra time off during the summer to match their kids' schedules can lose income, especially if they're paid hourly or they're self-employed. The other alternative, sending kids to summer camp, isn't cheap, to say the least.

And, when summer vacation's over, you've got tanned students who have probably forgotten a good chunk of what they learned before the break, as I did each year with math. Finally, when students graduate, they enter the workforce having been conditioned for years to think of the summer months as downtime. Being disorganized and unproductive between Memorial Day and Labor Day have become engrained habits.

Once again, because we're continuing to follow a system outdated long ago by societal and technological advances, we're adding layers of stress and dysfunction to our lives. Yet we're so accustomed to that stress and dysfunction, we don't even see it, or know where it comes from.

Through the years, there have been efforts to tweak the summer vacation from school. For example, some American schools have experimented with the "forty-five–fifteen" model, whereby nine-week school terms alternate with three-week vacations throughout the year.[11] In this model, one group of kids is on vacation during any given week. Advocates say schools following the forty-five–fifteen schedule are less crowded. Kids get better attention from teachers and staff, while schools still serve the same number of students. But many parents want their kids off during the entire summer season,[12] despite all these downsides I mentioned, so the forty-five–fifteen model has never really caught on.

What's the answer to the summer vacation dilemma? Sorry; again, I don't have one. It's a far larger problem than any one person can take on. But we can begin to figure out a solution by asking ourselves some important questions. Does it make sense to have all students taking the exact same period of time off? What if schools ran throughout the year, with minibreaks here and there? What impact might a fresh approach to the school calendar have on your life, your family's time together, and, most importantly, your child's education? Or, to put it more bluntly, wouldn't it make more sense to organize schools around how we want people to learn, instead of around the outdated assumption that students need time off for farming?

And so, much of how our educational system is organized is wrong for what we need today. We're more or less stuck with this system for now. It's simply too entrenched for us to expect that it will change in the near future. But, also like the nine-to-five workday, there are things you can do to mitigate its negative effects on you and your family. If you have young kids, you could organize a summer playgroup for children in your neighborhood, rotating the supervision duties among the parents. You might arrange to work from home several days a week over the summer, reducing your commute time and allowing you to keep an eye on the young ones too. And there's always summer school (though this option will undoubtedly give the kids something else to hold against you later).

Your Fast Car Is Stuck in Traffic

Few technological advances have had a bigger impact on our society than the car. And the car, together with the societal structures it inadvertently created, is high on my list of what's wrong in our world today.

The car changed everything: how and where we live, work, shop, play, and pray. The whole thing started with a German named Karl Benz (the second half of Mercedes-Benz) who invented the first practical automobile in 1885[13] (it was a three-wheeler, but hey, you have to start somewhere).

Over time, the early models became more modern (with four wheels, even) and affordable. Pretty soon, most families in America had one car, if not several.

Once we could travel longer distances faster and more conveniently than ever before, we started living farther and farther from city centers. But the communities the automobile created didn't take into account problems that developed later, such as dependency on foreign oil, global warming, and traffic congestion. And yet, we keep building, moving into, and living in these commuter

> You got a fast car / But is it fast enough so we can fly away?
> —Tracy Chapman, "Fast Car"

communities, even though they harm our planet and add stress to our lives.

Originally, the car was marketed as a machine that would set us free and, by getting us places faster, give us excess leisure time (doesn't that sound familiar?). But talk about the Law of Unintended Consequences: The car also did a hit-and-run on downtown city centers, which went onto life support as suburbia sprouted everywhere.

Ah, suburbia. Where else can you live surrounded by people just like you, in houses that look just like yours? The irony is that you probably don't even know these people because you enter and leave your house through your garage, your houses are spaced far apart, and everyone's too busy to stop and chat anyway.

From the car we got the Interstate Highway System, which the Eisenhower administration launched in 1956.[14] Thanks to the highway, we could live even farther away from the people we actually know—parents, grandparents, hometown buddies, business associates.

Don't get me wrong. I love my car as much as you love yours. But let's be clear: The automobile scattered our lives over miles of freeways and streets. Add to this the nine-to-five workday, plus school and day care schedules, and you get gridlock, which is an incredible drain on productivity and a major source of stress. Think of it this way: We spend an average of fifty-two minutes each day just getting to work and back.[15] That's over four hours a week—half of an eight-hour workday—spent sitting in a car.

We're making progress, of course. As gas prices rise, so does interest in *smart growth* planning, whereby communities closely cluster businesses, homes, stores, schools, and churches. In an interesting reversal of the urban flight that took place in the 1960s and 1970s, there's a growing trend of people moving back into downtown city centers. And more of us are working from home, at least part of the time. These are all positive developments. But our current structures took decades to develop, and they'll take decades to change.

Of course, we'll never get rid of cars entirely. But we can come up with creative ways to use them less. For example, the Italian city of Lecco came up with a clever way to get school buses off the road and reduce automobile use; they organized and financed *piedibus* routes.[16] *Piedibus* literally translates from Italian to "foot bus." The idea, proposed by a local environmental group, was to encourage schoolchildren to walk to school along planned routes with adult supervision so they wouldn't have to be driven by their parents. The *piedibus* was conceived to counter three negative societal trends, each of which can be traced at least partly to the automobile: traffic congestion, carbon dioxide emissions, and childhood obesity. A success in Italy, the *piedibus* concept (under different names) has spread to parts of France, Britain, and the United States. It's a classic example of how people can work together to overcome the problems our technological advances inadvertently create.

Once Upon a Time, When Knowledge Was Power

Frederick W. Taylor wouldn't have characterized his innovation of scientific management as bad for society or individuals. He'd have said that scientific management made it possible for as many people as possible to have good jobs and succeed at them. But he was reacting to a different worldview—and a different world—in which knowledge was power and was hard to acquire.

Once upon a time, knowledge *was* power. At a time when knowledge wasn't easily available or disseminated—before the printing press, before schools were everywhere, before most people could read—and only a few possessed it, knowledge was a hot commodity.

To show you what I mean, imagine that it's the 1600s, and you've decided to become a stonemason. You start as an apprentice toiling at the knee of a master stonemason. Instead of paying you, the master artisan teaches you his trade. He feeds and shelters you in his home. He works you constantly. The master stonemason can get away with this. He's the only one with the knowledge you need to put food in your mouth. Because of his knowledge, he has power. You don't.

About seven years later,[17] your apprenticeship is finished. It's time to advance to the next stage: a journeyman stonemason. Maybe you're now an employee of the master stonemason's. Or you travel between villages, honing your skills and building more knowledge. More years pass. Finally, you have the knowledge to become a master stonemason. Good for you. Now *you* have power. You're ready to take on an apprentice of your own, pass along your knowledge to the next generation, and, given the brief life spans in those days, promptly expire.

And so the cycle went, for decades. Then came movable type. When printing presses began cranking out books and later newspapers and magazines, knowledge was no longer so easily contained. The printed word transformed our societies in ways we couldn't have anticipated.

Over time, published information became available on any imaginable topic. It rapidly became cheaper and easier for the average person to get that information. Once schools started to proliferate and more children learned to read, new opportunities began to appear. You didn't have to be a stonemason if you didn't want to. You could learn another trade, and you didn't have to learn it from the one master in the village. Knowledge was spreading, and those who had it were no longer in the minority—which means they weren't as powerful as they once had been.

Through the years, new forms of mass media, including radio, newspapers, television, and the Internet, distributed knowledge ever further (though not everyone would use *television* and *knowledge* in the same sentence). As a result, people began to develop ever more highly specialized knowledge and expertise they believed would continue to give them power.

But there's a problem with that scenario too. Today, when most people in developed nations have easy access to information from around the world, communication costs are cheap, and we have plenty of education options, even specialized knowledge doesn't necessarily give you power. In fact, you may not even have to develop your own knowledge anymore. Just go on Google and borrow someone else's. (I'm not talking about skill in this context, by the way. There will always be value in how you use the knowledge you acquire. I'm talking about the acquisition of knowledge itself.)

In other words, knowledge was power when it wasn't readily available and when apprenticeship was the primary way to acquire it. But in an era of widespread, inexpensive communications, knowledge simply spreads too rapidly for it to hold power for long. So there's no point in trying to cram a ton of it into your head. A much better strategy is to have a system for storing and organizing knowledge, so you can access or recall it when you need it (more specifics on how to do this in Part Two).

If this were a lecture instead of a book, I'd ask for a show of hands now: How many of you believe or have believed your knowledge gives you power? Once I finished counting hands—and if you're all being honest, it will take me a minute—I'd have to sheepishly raise mine. I've been caught in that trap myself. And it put me in the hospital.

The Bell Rang, My Blood Vessels Burst

Back in January 2004, I was the chief information officer at Google, a position I'd had for a few months. Late one Friday afternoon, after I'd left for the day, I received a call from George Reyes, Google's CFO at the time.

"I need you to come to a meeting," George said.

"Sure," I answered. "When?" I was leaving for Europe the following Monday for my best friend's wedding as well as for business.

"Can you make it *now*?"

I sighed, said good-bye to the friends I was with, and headed back to the office. The meeting was already in progress in a conference room full of investment bankers, George, and some other Google staffers. Everyone was abuzz about this "crazy" idea Google cofounder Larry Page had about taking the company public. They wanted to know: *Can* we make this happen?

The discussion got technical. I was asked detailed questions about what technology would be involved in such an undertaking. All eyes were on me. As I spoke, I began to believe that in this extremely important area, I had unique knowledge (that is, power). And, given that I was a fairly new hire, I also wanted to prove my value to my colleagues.

So I expanded my role in the initial public offering (IPO) effort. For months, I worked two jobs: the one I was hired to do and the one I had assumed related to the IPO. During the six months it took Google to go public, I didn't eat properly or exercise regularly, if at all. At least three nights a week, I crashed, exhausted, in a hotel room near Google's Mountain View headquarters. I struggled to sleep, only to drag myself back to work first thing the next morning even more tired than I'd been the day before. Oh, and I experienced lots of crazy-intense headaches and vertigo too. And before it was all over, I'd lost about thirty-five pounds. Let's just say the "Pre-IPO Weight Loss Plan" is not one I'd recommend. In short: I was a mess.

Finally, a colleague suggested I could use some help. He quickly put together a small team to support me. I felt like a jungle explorer in an old movie who was sinking in quick-sand, and someone had just thrown me a vine. But in my heart, I didn't believe I needed it.

I did.

Heroes die off every day.

—Lagwagon, "The Kids Are All Wrong"

Fast-forward to August 19, 2004. I was among the company's team members present for the bell ringing at the Nasdaq stock exchange in New York to kick off Google's first day as a publicly traded company. It was an exhilarating experience, to have finally reached the end of this particularly long and winding road.

Later that day, two female colleagues and I were leaving for the airport. As I clambered into the back of the car, both women looked at me with unconcealed alarm, as if my eyes were bleeding. One of them handed me her compact mirror. I took a look. As it turned out, my eyes *were* bleeding. Blood vessels in both eyes had burst.

I returned to California. After a hospital visit or two, I was diagnosed with an autoimmune disorder, which I hadn't known I had until the months of stress pushed it to the surface. I changed my diet, got some rest, and returned to normal (what-

THE RINGING OF THE BELL

The Nasdaq "bell ringing" isn't all that impressive, to be honest. In fact, Nasdaq doesn't even have a trading floor.[18]

Nasdaq is an all-digital network, so it doesn't actually need a bell ringing to signify the start or end of share trading. The bell ringing is entirely ceremonial and designed to emulate the New York Stock Exchange's well-known tradition.

When you ring the Nasdaq bell, you're actually standing on a platform in a soundstage, crammed in between the various financial reporters doing their live reports. You push a button to "ring the bell," but the button doesn't actually do anything. It's all a camera-ready illusion.

ever that means). When my head cleared, I realized the error in my thinking that had gotten me into this predicament. I'd mistakenly believed I was the only person with the knowledge and ability to coordinate the technology required to support one of the most hyped IPOs in recent history, which gave me a false sense of power and compelled me to take on way more work than I could handle. Added to that was arrogance and a desire to be a hero, and it's a wonder my entire brain didn't burst.

And that brings me to my sixth principle of organization: *Knowledge is not power. The* sharing *of knowledge is power.* It's a fallacy to think you're the only one in your company or department who has specific knowledge, and therefore a certain power.

> Knowledge is not power. The *sharing* of knowledge is power.

Whatever task you're trying to complete, or whatever part of your life you're trying to organize, you'll be far more successful—and way less stressed—when you share knowledge rather than hoard it. Think about it: Two people collectively know more than one; three know more than two; and when you have a room full of smart people willing to share their knowledge, there's very little you can't accomplish together.

I believe this is a far better approach than working crazy hours to build your "unique" knowledge or to show everyone you're the only one with that special knowledge. Go build a team instead. Figure out what you're good at, and be honest about what you're lousy at. Delegate what you're not good at to others and trust them to do their jobs. Even better, always try to work with people who are smarter than you, whose backgrounds, perspectives, and skills are different from yours. Share what you know and encourage them to do the same. You'll learn from them. They'll learn from you. You'll all do a better job. Isn't that what you should be working toward in the first place?

It's Not About Working Harder

To put this all into perspective, concern about being organized is a luxury—and a curse—of an affluent, technologically advanced society. Cave dwellers didn't fret about being organized. All they worried about was how not to be eaten by big animals. Back in the 1850s, when the United States was on the brink of the Civil War, everyday folks didn't wring their hands about being disorganized, either.

Even so, given the complex society we live in today, we need to figure out how to be better organized, or we'll flounder. We need to work together with people who differ from us, so we can find creative solutions to huge challenges.

The world's changing at an accelerated pace. Our employers expect us to do more in less time—and to do it with fewer resources, especially during an economic recession. At the same time, completing each task requires us to process and deal with a higher volume of information than ever before. And in the meantime, our brains and our societal structures are ill suited for the ways in which we live and work.

The good news is that technology makes it possible to surmount many of these challenges. But, I believe, we have only begun to understand the endless ways in which technology can help us be more efficient, productive, and organized. We may have the means to keep up with the pace of the world, but we're still lagging because we haven't sufficiently challenged our old, outdated models of doing things.

The solution isn't to work harder. You're already doing that. Instead, what you really want to do is work smarter—to use the tools and technology available to get around the constraints society imposes.

But first, it's important to identify and own up to your own psychological, emotional, or other constraints, which is the topic of the next chapter. Once you do that, you can begin to change how you *react* to them, and, thus, you can minimize their impact on you. The next chapter will help you learn how to identify your constraints so you can organize around them, instead of ignoring them. And then you can begin to make right some of the things in your world that are wrong.

ENCODE THIS

- Many of the most established structures and beliefs in our world are all wrong, from the nine-to-five workday to summer breaks from school, to the assumptions we make about the power of knowledge. Each makes organization more difficult.

- Too often, we try to make our lives work within outdated structures, rather than revise the structures to work within our lives. The end result is that, every day, we're doing things wrong. It's not our fault. But by doing things wrong, we're taxing our brain and adding stress to our lives, which keeps us from being better organized.

- The good news is, we're not powerless. But in order to thrive, we first must question our structures. We may not be able to change them dramatically. But we can work around them by changing how we react to them and minimizing their impact on us. Some things you can do:

- Try to anticipate how technology might change your life, instead of ignoring those changes after they're entrenched.

- Take advantage of affordable, abundant technology (such as fast Internet access and videoconferencing) to work at home, at least part of the time.

- Talk to your boss about switching your hours to avoid traffic congestion.

- If you have young kids, organize a summer playgroup for children in your neighborhood, rotating the supervision duties among the parents.

- Send the kids to summer school (though this is likely to make you wildly unpopular).

- Consider moving closer to work, school, church, and shopping, to minimize time and resources wasted driving long distances.

- Don't buy into the knowledge-is-power trap. Share your knowledge with others and invite them to do the same. Everyone does a better job that way.

- Work with others—preferably people who are different from you—to find manageable solutions to some of the bigger problems in your world.

chapter 3

RACECARS, BASKETBALL SHORTS & OPERA

owning up to our personal constraints

SO FAR, I'VE DESCRIBED constraints everyone faces. Our brain, and how it limits what we remember and what we can do, is a big one. Others come from outdated assumptions and societal structures, such as nine-to-five workdays and summer breaks from school.

But that's not the whole story. You and I each have constraints that are specific to us and that can prevent us from being organized and successful. In this chapter, I'll help you avoid this by showing you how to identify your specific constraints and develop strategies to work around them.

Here's an example of the kind of personal constraint I'm talking about. I love automobile racing and I would be a Formula 1 racecar driver, if only I could. But that's not going to happen. One reason is that I'm too tall, and there's not much I can do about that. More importantly, I'm too slow. I can't make myself respond at lightning speeds, not even with massive caffeine injections. Alas, there goes another dream into the dustbin.

But enough about me. Let's talk about you. What are your personal constraints? Maybe you're a chronic procrastinator or an obsessive overachiever. Could be you're always second-guessing yourself, you're way too easily distracted, or you have an exceptionally poor memory. Or maybe you're dyslexic, like me. These are just a few of the many personal challenges that can hold you back from being organized at work and in your personal life. But they don't have to.

The problem with constraints is they're so…constraining. They have a nasty habit of blocking us from achieving our goals. So in order to be better organized, it's important to fully understand your constraints and challenges: where they come from; whether they're real or assumed, inherent or inherited; how they affect you and your ability to achieve your goals; and what you can realistically do about them. When you don't honestly own up to your constraints, you waste time, effort, money, and energy doing things you don't need to do or aren't capable of doing well. You screw up, and then it's into the downward stress spiral you go.

> God grant me the serenity to accept the things I cannot change, courage to change the things I can, and wisdom to know the difference.
>
> —The Serenity Prayer, often attributed to Reinhold Niebuhr

Some constraints are absolutely within our control to change or overcome. Others, like my height, are completely beyond our control, but they can be worked around.

In general, there are two broad classes of constraints: *assumed* and *actual*. Many of our limitations seem real.

Maybe they are. But maybe they aren't. Perhaps you just assume they're real based on past experience, history, what others have told you, or the structures of society. This chapter is about learning to identify, accept, and work around your *actual* constraints so you won't waste time and energy on things you can't change.

Assumed Versus Actual

Let's begin with my seventh principle of organization: *Organize around actual constraints, not assumed ones.*

> ## Organize around actual constraints, not assumed ones.

Easy enough, right? Not exactly. Identifying your actual constraints requires a dash of soul searching, some input from people you trust, and a touch of fearlessness. But it's well worth the efforts.

Whether something is an actual constraint for you can depend upon many factors. Context is one. For example, my height prevents me from becoming a racecar driver. So in that context my height is an actual constraint. But it wouldn't be if my goal were to be a professional basketball player. My aversion to wearing basketball shorts in public is a constraint that can't possibly be overcome, however.

Relevance to your life is another. What may be an actual constraint for one person may be only an assumed constraint for you. As I mentioned in chapter 2, many of us continue to follow or are significantly affected by the nine-to-five workday tradition. This tradition evolved from a constraint—the need to organize workers on an assembly line—that doesn't affect most of us anymore. Thus, the nine-to-five workday may be an *actual* constraint for people who work in a factory. There's really nothing they can do about it, other than find another job.

To you, the nine-to-five workday may *seem* like an actual

constraint. Your company expects you to be there from nine to five for various reasons. But in truth, many companies don't really need all their workers in the office from nine to five anymore—they just think they do. And so, if you stop and think about it, isn't the nine-to-five workday, Monday–Friday workweek, actually an *assumed* constraint for you?

Sometimes, we're held back by constraints that don't exist for us at all. We were simply told they existed, and we believed it. The world is full of heartbreaking stories stemming from the wrongful assumption that a constraint is real when it's not.

True story: A woman in her early eighties was recently talking about opera to my coauthor Jim. "When I was younger," she said, "I wanted to be a professional opera singer. But my teacher told me I wasn't good enough, so I never tried."

The woman did, however, have a tape of herself singing a particularly famous aria, which had been recorded on tape over forty years earlier. She played the tape for Jim. Her singing was powerful and beautiful. Had the teacher not handed her this constraint, and had she not accepted it at face value, Jim's friend might well have had a successful career as an opera singer.

Of course, each of us has plenty of actual constraints, which are real no matter how you look at them. An actual constraint is one that truly does impose limitations on you, in some way. You aren't simply assuming you have that limitation, and you're not just accepting at face value a constraint handed to you by society, your spouse, a teacher, or anyone else.

An actual constraint generally involves something you have absolutely no control over. It might be small and fleeting: You've got only ten minutes to get to the FedEx drop-off location before it closes. You arrive just in time, only to discover the store has closed a few minutes early. Game over. Short of racing to the airport to try to catch the last FedEx flight out before it leaves, there's nothing you can do. Maybe the concern is money. You have a big monthly mortgage payment, you've just been laid off with only one month's sever-ance, and it's a brutal job market. Either way, these are real constraints that, at the moment you're facing them at least, you have no control over. However, given a little time, there are things you can do to work around them, or to minimize their impact.

Whatever your constraints might be, the first step is to identify them as such. Take a few minutes and write down all the constraints you can identify that are keeping you from being productive and organized. Next, try to determine if the challenges you've identified are actual or assumed. Trust me: This isn't easy.

A Panoramic View of You

The tricky thing about constraints is that, even though we may think we know what ours are, we're often wrong. We're really bad at objectively evaluating ourselves and our envi-ronments. For example, most of us believe we're better than average at common tasks, like driving or managing people. But we can't *all* be better than average. If we were, the aver-age would have to be much higher.

On the other hand, if tasks are particularly difficult or unusual, we often think we're worse than average. Let me assure you, you're no more inept at connecting home theater components than your neighbor. If we can't all be better than average, it follows that we can't all be worse than average either.

We also tend to believe we have more control over what happens to us than we actually do. Gamblers often exhibit this fallacy. Have you ever been so "lucky" at the table that you didn't want to give up the dice? You just *knew* you were going to win the next roll. Sometimes you did, sometimes you didn't, but the point is that fate controlled the dice, not you.

So given the tricks our minds play on us, how do we deter-mine what our actual constraints are? We start with my eighth principle of organization: *Be completely honest—but never judgmental—with yourself.*

> **Be completely honest—but never judgmental—with yourself.**

A quick aside: When we're not honest with ourselves, we complicate our lives (and often the lives of those around us) needlessly. Being honest with ourselves—and with others—is not only the right thing to do; it's a great way to save time and energy. Think about it: One lie begets another, and another, and another. Pretty soon, you have to remember what you said and to whom. You spend a lot of mental power protecting a lie. Honestly, wouldn't that mental capacity be better spent on something more productive?

Okay, back to our previously scheduled program: To determine what your actual constraints might be, you could try a technique on yourself that's frequently used in the corporate world: the *360 performance review*. That's when your coworkers, subordinates, and supervisor offer their feedback on your job performance—what you're doing well, or poorly, your strengths and weaknesses, and so on. (The "360" refers to a 360-degree, panoramic view.)

Granted, these aren't exactly fun to do, but a third-party perspective can often be eye-opening. Talk to your spouse, close friends, colleagues, or others who'll offer you their honest opinions. Even your kids might have some interesting comments (kids tend to be painfully honest). Ask people you trust what they see as your strengths and weaknesses; you could even read them that list you just made and ask them to tell you honestly which constraints *they* think apply. You may hear some of the same things repeated by several people, which will help you uncover patterns of behavior that cause you to "get in your own way."

> I follow where my mind goes.
> —The Psychedelic Furs, "Love My Way"

I realize this approach may seem intimidating or overwhelming. If so, try taking a baby step first. Are you "churning" in a project—doing things over and over and getting nowhere? Ask just one person, someone you trust and who will be honest, for feedback. You might describe to him or her the challenge you're facing and your suspicions about what's making this particular task or project so difficult, and ask whether he or she agrees.

I'll give you an example of how helpful a third-party perspective can be. When I was in graduate school, I had to write papers for conferences and journals. One paper I was trying to write was about a particular experiment I'd just completed. I had a topic and an assigned word count. I clearly understood the paper's goals, as well as my own. And I knew the material cold.

But for some reason, I struggled to get the thing done. I knew something was wrong, but I didn't know what, so I set aside the paper to get some distance from it. When that yielded no insights, I asked some folks around me, including an editor who'd spent many years leading one of the most respected journals in my field, what they thought was holding me back. The editor's advice was simple, honest, and insightful: "You're writing to look smart. Just write to be clear."

The editor had identified a constraint I couldn't see at first; I *was* trying too hard to appear smart to the reader. Because of that desire, I wrote extremely long, convoluted, erudite sentences that were full of twenty-five-cent words, like *erudite*. My writing was so "smart" that it was practically unreadable.

I went back to work on my paper, this time writing shorter, clearer prose. While my constraint was very real, by stepping back, being honest with myself, and asking for help, I was able to identify and overcome it.

By the way, the paper was published. Thanks for asking.

How else can you get a panoramic view of yourself and of which limitations are real and which aren't? You could look back at other projects you've completed recently (and I don't just mean projects at work—I'm talking about personal projects too). Where did you succeed? Where could you have done a better job? What would you do differently now? If you examine how you performed two or more projects, you may find patterns that offer insights into where you tend to trip yourself up.

Also, pay particular attention to what scares, stresses, frustrates, and angers you. If you're like me, you experience those emotions when you're being squeezed by one or more constraints. The more intensely you feel those emotions, the bigger the constraint may be.

It's also important to take an honest look at your environment. What are the actual roadblocks (versus the assumed ones) the world throws in your path on a regular basis? For example, do you never have enough time to do everything your boss expects of you? If so, why not? Is it because you aren't managing your time well? Or maybe you've agreed to take on more than is humanly possible, in an effort to please your boss? Remember, if you don't know what the problem is, you can't solve it.

Can You Control It?

Okay, you've identified your constraints, and you've separated the false ones from the real ones. At this point, it helps to dig just a little deeper. You want to determine which of your actual constraints are within your control, and which ones aren't. Why? Because you don't want to waste time and energy trying to change something you can't.

Some limitations can't be overcome. All you can do is organize around them, in hopes of minimizing their effect. For example, no matter how hard you try, there will never be more than twenty-four hours in a day or seven days in a week. Even more of a bummer, time will eventually run out for you, as it will for me. For both of our sakes, I hope that's not for a long time. Meanwhile, we have to accept time as something we can't change, be realistic about its impact on our goals, and plan accordingly.

> **Time keeps on slippin', slippin', slippin' / Into the future.**
>
> —The Steve Miller Band, "Fly Like an Eagle"

There are other constraints beyond the control of most people. In my case, it's dyslexia. There's no pill or medical treatment that will make it disappear. However, that doesn't mean I'm powerless to change its impact on me.

For example, because of my dyslexia, I have an extremely poor sense of direction. One way to deal with this challenge would be to stumble around unaided, assuming that through trial and error or repetition, I would learn my way eventually.

But instead, I enlist as much help as I can to get me where I'm going. I'm lucky enough to have friends who help me get places by driving me or by navigating. Technology helps me work around this constraint too. I have GPS systems in my car, on my motorcycle, and on my phone to give me directions. And there are plenty of online mapping services, which I use often.

If all these fail, I have a backup plan: I count turns. If I'm going somewhere new, I pay attention to how I'm getting there—a left turn, go two blocks, make a right, go to the stop sign, turn left. Then, when returning, I reverse the turns. This trick usually works because I'm organizing *around* a constraint—my dyslexia—instead of fighting it, ignoring it, or denying its impact.

However, working around a constraint isn't always easy. Sometimes constraints beyond our control lurk just beneath the surface of those you *can* control, and vice versa. What if you've identified your long commute to work as a major constraint? You could move closer to work, or perhaps you could work from home several days a week. But you can't afford to sell your home and buy another one right now, so that leaves working from home. Unfortunately, your boss won't allow you to do that (he being one of those untrusting types). His stubbornness may be out of your control, but this doesn't mean you don't have other options. For example, you could find new ways to be productive during your commute: Use your laptop on the train, listen to business books on tape in your car, and so on. The key is to always be on the lookout for new and creative ways to work around roadblocks and limitations, whenever possible.

The constraints that stem from your emotions can be the most difficult ones to identify and control, but it can be done. Maybe you chronically overcommit because you have low self-esteem and don't know how to say no, or want to be seen as a hero. This becomes a big, ongoing obstacle to being organized because you'll always have more on your to-do list than you could possibly accomplish.

Whatever the constraint, you have to face your own behaviors, actions, desires, and emotions honestly. While this may sound a bit touchy-feely, consider this: Greek tragedies typically featured heroes who self-destructed because they didn't honestly examine themselves. Clearly, our resistance to frank self-evaluation has been going on for a really long time.

> **All we need is just a little patience.**
> —Guns N' Roses, "Patience"

Knowing When to Ignore a Constraint

Identifying and organizing around your constraints, however, isn't without some risk. It's possible to give them *too* much thought and weight. Even if your constraints are real and beyond your control, that doesn't mean you should give up on the task at hand. When you do that, you don't leave space for new ideas, experiences, and outcomes. That's why it's important to keep my ninth principle of organization in mind: *Know when to ignore your constraints.*

> **Know when to ignore your constraints.**

For an example, let's return to the world of professional racecar driving. In 1995, a seventy-year-old man was among the members of a team competing in the Rolex 24 at Daytona, a twenty-four-hour endurance race. No doubt, the driver understood that his age would be a major constraint (one he obviously couldn't control) toward achieving his goal. No one remotely close to his age had ever won in that event before.[1] Even so, he went for it anyway. And his team won. By the way, you may have heard of this guy. His name was Paul Newman.

But how do you know when to ignore a constraint? You

weigh it against your assets, such as your skills, available resources, and the help you can get from others. You also take into consideration the risks: What's the worst thing that can happen if you ignore a constraint? Newman's age was certainly a constraint, but it was also an asset; his age also gave him many years of experience driving racecars. Previously, he'd won several racing events, so it wasn't ridiculous to think he had at least a chance of helping his team score the Rolex 24 championship. And as a member of a team, he had excellent resources to help him.

Earlier I mentioned emotional constraints we impose on ourselves. When you think about it, fear is probably the biggest one we all face. In this example, Newman wasn't held back by fear of failing, or of looking foolish, or of anything else. That's an important lesson. More often than not, fear is a constraint best ignored.

The Constraints of Stress

Feeling stressed is itself a huge constraint, however temporary it might be at the time. When you're under an extraordinary amount of stress, you often can't think rationally, and you're likely to make an already challenging situation even worse.

I have an example from my own life, one that I'll return to again at various points in this book. It's a particularly painful story to share, but I hope it will help shed some light for you on the importance of being organized, so that you're better equipped to face the unexpected, when it strikes.

A few years ago, before I met Sonya, I was living with a woman named Jeanne. We'd met when we both worked at Charles Schwab. One day, I was settling into my seat in a large meeting when I noticed a beautiful blonde, with bright blue eyes, pearl white skin, and a quirky smile. This unknown coworker was stunning, well dressed, and had a hint of mischief in her eyes. She waved at me from across the room, and then she ducked behind the person she was seated next to, suddenly shy.

It wasn't long before I fell in love with this lovely, kind, gentle woman with the wicked sense of humor and the high-heel shoes. Jeanne always wanted pearls and a Jaguar. She loved dogs, hated injustice, and thought there was always time to shop. A younger coworker once cattily denounced Jeanne as a blonde bimbo. Jeanne, who had earned a Ph.D. and had enjoyed a successful career at General Electric, Andersen Consulting, and Schwab, was the first to laugh at the put-down. She loved the fact that some twenty-something was jealous of her.

Looking on / She sings the songs.

—Elton John, "Tiny Dancer"

Jeanne and I shared a love of music. She'd been a singer in a local band, and she loved the music she sang: Aimee Mann, the Pretenders, and most of all, Elton John. As a teenager in Indiana, she used to sit in her room for hours, singing along to his records on a portable turntable, dreaming of his voice and of the stories he told, feeling free and safe.

At the time we met, Jeanne had two dogs: Minnie, a Dalmatian she rescued from death row in an animal shelter, and Tyrone, a Labrador retriever mix someone had abandoned in a cardboard box outside a grocery store. I came to love the dogs almost as much as I loved Jeanne.

Then, in February 2006, Jeanne was diagnosed with cancer of the bile duct.

One night, during those horrible months of her illness, she had an emergency that required an ambulance to take her to a local hospital to get stabilized. Once stable, she was transferred to Stanford University hospital, where she'd been receiving all her care.

But I didn't go with her to get her settled in at Stanford. I was tired and wanted to get some sleep. Not only was this selfish, of course, but it was also a major mistake. When I left, in a misguided attempt to be helpful, I took her clothes and purse with me.

In the event you ever face this situation, trust me: This is not a smart strategy. In Jeanne's purse were her most important documents: her patient medication card and her health care power of attorney form. These documents were crucial to getting checked into intensive care properly. We both knew she needed those documents. But we were extraordinarily stressed, upset (and if those aren't huge constraints, I don't know what is), and we simply weren't thinking clearly. And my bone-headed decision to take her clothes and purse with me only caused extra hassles and exacerbated Jeanne's stress level—the last thing she needed.

Admittedly, it's extremely difficult to think rationally when you're helping a spouse or partner through a crisis like a terminal illness. Your own personal constraints—in my case, a tendency to forget things—tend to become magnified when stress is so high, which usually leads to outcomes, like this one, that cause even more stress. That's why it's so important to identify and have strategies in place for working around your constraints well *before* something hugely challenging happens. It's also helpful to surround yourself with other people who can think clearly and who aren't stressed like you. I'll talk more about that in the next chapter.

ENCODE THIS

- Whether they're physical, psychological, or imposed on us by society, we all have constraints particular to us.

- To be better organized, it's important to fully understand your constraints and challenges: where they come from, whether they're actual or assumed, how they affect you, and what you can realistically do about them.

- There are two broad categories of constraints: *assumed* constraints that may or may not be real, and *actual* constraints that *are* real. It's essential to know the difference, so you don't waste time and energy trying to overcome a constraint that doesn't exist.

- It's hard to know what our actual constraints are because we're really bad at objectively evaluating ourselves and our environments. That's when we need to ask others for help.

- Of the constraints that *are* real, some are within our control. Others can be mitigated but not entirely overcome. Still others are completely out of our control. The sooner we figure out which those are, the sooner we can stop wasting time on things that aren't going to yield positive results.

- Know when to ignore your constraints. Weigh the constraint against your assets, such as your skills and available resources. Consider what's at stake too. What's the worst that can happen if you ignore the constraint? Whatever you decide, try not to let irrational fear take control. Fear is an emotional constraint that's often best ignored.

- It's important to identify and develop strategies to get around those constraints that flare up in times of stress *before* the unexpected happens. That way you'll be better prepared if a crisis should strike.

chapter 4

CLIMB THAT MOUNTAIN OR CHILL IN THE BARCALOUNGER?

the importance of having clear goals

IN THIS CHAPTER
Knowing What to Do, What Not to Do
Being Flexible
Going Blank
Making Decisions

WHEN I WAS STUDYING for a Ph.D. at Princeton, my advisor would edit my papers before we submitted them to conferences. At first, my drafts were often returned covered with so much red ink that I could barely make out what was written underneath. I'd slog through all the comments, make changes, and submit a revised draft—only to face another red tidal wave.

I felt completely overwhelmed. I wasn't making any progress, and my advisor wasn't giving me the feedback I needed to improve. Finally, after one of our multiple back-and-forth sessions, he scrawled across my paper, in enormous, all-capital scarlet letters:

His not-so-simple question about my question filled me with questions of my own. I wasn't entirely sure of anything at this point. When I asked him to explain, my advisor said I hadn't been clear about what I was trying to achieve as I wrote the paper. I should identify the goal of the paper right off the bat, he said, and write only with that goal in mind.

It was an important lesson for me, one that still guides me today. A clearly defined goal (and action plan to achieve it) gives context and purpose to everything you do, whether it's writing an academic paper, tackling an important new work assignment, or planning your spouse's surprise birthday party. In turn, the context and purpose help you organize the information and actions necessary to achieve that goal much more effectively.

Goals are the flip side of constraints. Constraints are about obstacles, and goals are about possibilities. Having a clear understanding of both is key to moving forward in a way that's more likely to bring you success with the least amount of stress and effort. To be organized, everything you do should flow from your goals while taking your real constraints into consideration.

And with those kernels of wisdom, I've just saved you the considerable cost of a Princeton Ph.D.

Starting with specific goals in mind may seem very Organization 101. But you'd be surprised how many people don't do it, or do it incorrectly. They're too busy *doing* to stop and think about what they're doing or why they're doing it. They assume they already know what their goals are and barrel ahead without challenging their assumptions. So my tenth principle of organization is: *Know exactly where you're going—and how you'll get there—before you start the engine.*

Know exactly where you're going—and how you'll get there—before you start the engine.

In this chapter, I'll help you figure out how to define your goals for the tasks and projects you're facing, both big and small. Then I'll show you how to start developing a plan to meet them.

Do you know where you're going to?

—Diana Ross, Theme from *Mahogany*

Knowing What to Do, What Not to Do

When you don't know your goals, how do you know what's important? And if you don't know what's important, how do you know what information you need? Let's take that one step further: If you don't know what information you need, you can't know what information to encode—like lessons learned from tasks you've completed. Thus, you're making it harder on yourself to be efficient and organized. When you don't encode the information you need, you can't recall it later. That means you often end up doing things you need to do poorly, or doing things you don't need to do at all.

Let me give you an example. In graduate school, I studied people who were learning to program computers. The first time the students attempted to solve a particular programming task, they struggled. Eventually, after struggling for a while, they'd finish the project. Some students weren't clear about their goals before they began trying to solve the programming challenges. So they just used trial and error, trying to find something, anything that worked.

As is usually the case in school and in life, when you encounter a challenge, it helps if you've solved a similar problem before. When that happens, you can apply the knowledge and experience you already have to solving the new challenge. But this is true only if you know what knowledge and experience is relevant to the task at hand. In this case, since the students hadn't been clear about what they were trying to do in the first programming project, they didn't know what to encode as they went along. They couldn't be sure which parts of their solution mattered and therefore should be reused and which parts of their solution actually got in their way of solving the new programming challenge. In other words, they hadn't decided what they were trying to achieve when they performed the first programming task.

As a result, for the second programming project, many students simply reused the entire solution they'd stumbled upon doing the first project, instead of using only the relevant pieces. Sometimes the reused bits of programming worked for solving the new task. But often, those bits introduced errors. More importantly, the students created unnecessary work for themselves. Without clearly articulated goals to guide them when doing the first programming task, they didn't know how to apply what they'd learned to the later one.

On the other hand, the more successful students set clear goals for themselves to achieve during the first programming tasks. So, later, they instinctively knew what information was relevant to their new goals. That information enabled them to reuse only those pieces of the solution that were appropriate, which allowed them to solve the problem a whole lot faster.

I want to emphasize the difference between the more successful students and the rest. The successful students weren't smarter, nor were they more experienced. They simply followed a better strategy: being clear about what they were doing and why they were doing it.

I realized from watching these students that being organized is partly about successfully recalling decisions made, experiments tried, and knowledge gained in the past. This doesn't mean you should blindly repeat what you've done before. In fact, most of the students who had trouble with the programming tasks were doing just that: reusing pieces of their solutions without any solid idea about why they had worked. Rather, the point is that you need to think about the *lessons* you've learned from tasks you've done before so you can more accurately judge how—or if—to apply that knowledge to new situations later. Setting clear goals from the start helps you do precisely that.

Being Flexible

As you can see, determining your goals before you begin a task or project is critical to success. Being specific about those goals is even more important. The more specific your goals are, the easier they are to achieve, and the easier your results are to measure.

That said, the *way* you achieve your goals doesn't necessarily need to be carved into stone. In fact, my eleventh principle of organization is: *Be flexible about how you achieve your goals*. Why? Because when we can't obtain our goals, we get frustrated and stressed. We may even give up. So I recommend being as specific as possible about your goals from the beginning, while also being open to seeing new ways to achieve them if your first approach fails. Let me put it this way: Be clear that you want to get from point *A* to point *B*. But also recognize there are a number of different routes you can take to get there.

> **Be flexible about how you achieve your goals.**

For example, a few years ago, I needed to relocate from the San Francisco Bay Area to Los Angeles, where I'd be working out of EMI's offices. I started off by setting several goals: Sell my home in the Bay Area; buy a new home in L.A.; hire movers; and so on.

I put my Bay Area home on the market and started shopping around in L.A. Along the way, a not-so-funny thing happened: The value of homes in the Bay Area, and much of the country, plunged.

> Let your mind go / Let yourself be free.
>
> —Aretha Franklin, "Think"

Nonetheless, I could have achieved the goal of selling my house—for significantly less than I thought it was worth. But something about the situation threw me into a tizzy, which told me I hadn't been clear enough in my original goal. It wasn't that I'd simply wanted to sell my home. I'd wanted to sell my home *for a certain price*. This may seem like a minor distinction. But the goal of selling my home for a certain price, I soon realized, involved a different set of actions and expectations than did the goal of simply selling my home.

Even as I refined my goal, I realized it wasn't obtainable in light of the market conditions at that time. Although disappointing, this realization was useful: Knowing I couldn't achieve my goal forced me to consider alternative solutions. And I soon found one that met my new vision.

Instead of selling my house, I rented it to a close friend who needed a place to live inexpensively. His goal was to save money for a down payment on a home. While I lost some money from the rent I charged, in the long run I'd have lost more had I sold my home at that time. Postponing the sale of my home allowed me to wait out the bottom of the real estate market. Best of all, I was able to help a friend, which made me feel good.

All told, it was the best possible outcome I could expect, given my specific goal and the declining residential real estate market (a constraint I was powerless to change). This outcome only occurred because I was flexible enough to revise the goals I'd set. Once I did that, I found a new, alternative way to get where I was going. Having an acceptable plan for an achievable goal is better than having an ideal plan for an impossible task.

> Where do we go from here ... And how do we spend our lives?
>
> —The Alan Parsons Project, "Games People Play"

Going Blank

By now, if you've been following (or at least humoring) me, you may have a little more self-awareness. You might have a clearer picture of the forces within you and in your environment that conspire to hold you back. You're beginning to understand how to define your specific goals.

Now you're ready to draw up plans that take into account your true constraints (and how you'll deal with them) as well as your specific goals. You're ready to tackle that big project or to-do list that's been keeping you up at night.

Cool. But please allow me, patient reader, to delay you for just another moment. Before diving in, set aside some time to clear your mind. Don't think about the problem or project you're facing. In fact, try not to think about anything at all.

Turn your mind into a blank sheet of paper, so you can get a fresh start.

When I'm about to face a particularly difficult challenge, I do something that forces my brain to stop churning: I ride my motorcycle. While riding, I can't focus on a problem in my head. I'm too busy keeping the bike moving and minding the traffic around me. Riding takes all my concentration. When I'm done, my mind is delightfully empty of worries.

> **Gotta keep rollin' / Gotta keep ridin'.**
>
> —Bob Seger, "Roll Me Away"

Whatever your preferred method is for clearing your head, it's important to start there. There are millions of ways to do this. Meditate. Practice yoga. Go for a walk. Sit in a park. Do something fun with your kids. Throw a ball for your dog.

Is your mind blank now? Perfect. Next, figure out whether you should, in fact, do the task you're considering at all. Does this particular mountain truly need climbing? Have others climbed it adequately before you? Did they take lots of pictures? If so, why do you need to whip out the pitons and follow in their path? Would your time be better spent chilling in your Barcalounger?

Fact is, someone, somewhere has probably already accomplished the task or solved the problem you're facing, or one similar to it. Starting from scratch or trying to reinvent the wheel is often a waste of precious time and brainpower. That's why, once I've set goals for a project, I look around to see if the problems I'll likely face have already been solved, and what elements of that solution I can adopt or borrow.

Sometimes, it turns out I've already solved the problem myself, or at least part of it. For instance, a while back I accepted an invitation to deliver a presentation on digital music at the Consumer Electronics Show. After determining what my goals were for the presentation, the next thing I did was review presentations I'd previously given on the topic, looking for talking points that were relevant to the new presentation I'd be giving. In other words, I started this new project by incorporating some relevant talking points from an earlier presentation, then building upon them with new research and perspectives.

Of course, we don't always have the luxury of borrowing from past solutions, as I did for this particular problem. So let's assume you've decided it's necessary to tackle a particular problem, from the beginning, with a blank slate. But what if it's a really challenging problem? That's okay. Life would be boring if we didn't have hard stuff to do. Your goal now should be to figure out what makes the problem so challenging. Maybe it's because you believe the constraints you've identified are beyond your control. But are you absolutely sure?

I'm a perennial optimist. The exciting thing about constraints you can't overcome is that sometimes, with help, you actually *can*. Perhaps all you need is the perspective of one other person, as I did when writing my paper. Maybe you need a team's help; that was true for me during the pre-IPO days at Google, even though I couldn't see it at first. And it was certainly true for me when Jeanne was ill.

Toward the end of Jeanne's struggle, she asked me if we could visit a warm beach. It took a small committee of people working together to enable me to take her, in fragile health, from our home in the Bay Area down to Santa Monica in Southern California. Ordinarily, planning such a trip wouldn't be difficult for me. But Jeanne's deteriorating health required us to take extra steps, and I was already overwhelmed and stressed, so I wasn't thinking clearly.

So without my having to ask, one friend cajoled reservations at a beachside hotel that was difficult to book in advance, much less on short notice. Another friend arranged her vacation time so she'd be near Santa Monica just in case I needed help while Jeanne and I were there. Each of them put their particular organizational skills to work, so all I'd have to do was pin down the dates. I have no idea what I did to deserve friends like them, but I'm grateful.

Anyhow, if, after personal reflection and getting feedback and help from others, you determine that the constraints holding you back are insurmountable, that's okay too. You shouldn't waste hours or days on something that isn't going anywhere. In this case, you should either alter your goals or delegate the task to someone better suited to handle it. This, in a nutshell, is why it's so important to truly understand your constraints as well as your goals. When you know what you're good at and what you're not good at, you're more likely to seek help with the latter instead of floundering.

Of course, enlisting others in your goals sometimes means delegating tasks to them (or if they're family members, guilt-tripping them). Delegation involves trust. You must trust the other person to do what you've asked. You may even have to teach the person how to do it. And if that's the case, sometimes delegating may feel like a lot of work that you could just as easily do yourself. (How many times have you thought, "In the time it will take me to explain this, I could just do it myself"?) That's not a good long-term strategy. For one thing, you're denying the other person the opportunity to learn something new or take on more responsibility. You may even be falling into that dreaded knowledge-is-power trip. But worse, if you don't learn to delegate, you can't free yourself up to focus on what's truly important *for you* to do.

Making Decisions

Now it's time to develop a plan of action. The plan should be designed to achieve your goals in a way that takes into account the actual constraints relevant to the project. It should include the specific actions that need to be taken, which are then matched to a timetable and to the available resources (in terms of people, time, money, and materials).

Of course, developing a plan requires making decisions. What are your priorities? What needs to be done, when, and by whom? How will you get the resources you've identified? In order to get the project done by the deadline, what will have to fall off the to-do list?

The bigger the plan, the bigger and more numerous your decisions are likely to be. But remember chapter 1? In addition to being fairly poor at evaluating our own limitations, we're quite bad at making decisions.

> I'm gonna make my own mistakes.
>
> —Lindsay Lohan, "I Decide"

Fortunately, we can learn to overcome, or at least compensate for, our poor decision-making skills. One way is simply to acknowledge them and try to recognize when they—and not you—are in control. Another way is to involve others. As I've mentioned before, I like to bounce my decisions off someone whose opinion I trust. That person usually helps me detect some faulty logic behind a decision. Or he or she will reinforce that I've made a good one.

You could do what Sonya does: Try the various outcomes of your decision on for size. Visualizing the possible results of your decision helps you clarify what you really want.

Research helps too. If you're feeling stuck, go online and get additional information. Try to find articles, blogs, or other information offered by others who've faced a challenge or a goal similar to yours. You can overdo this, of course, and overwhelm yourself with too much information. That makes your decision harder, not easier. So spend a little time gathering information online from a few select sources you trust, but don't obsess about it.

If you're really stuck, make a list of the pros and cons of whatever action you're considering. This may not sound like a novel idea, but, hey, if people have been doing it for years, maybe that's because it works. Try to prioritize the pros and cons in order of importance. If you want to get all mathematical about it, you could assign numeric values: 5 being extremely important, and 1 being extremely unimportant. Then add up the numbers for each of the pros and cons and see what you get. Sounds geeky, I know. But it can help.

You're not mathematically inclined? That makes two of us. Okay, try writing down your entire arguments in favor of and opposed to the decision you're considering. As you write, pay particular attention to your assumptions. Are they valid?

After you've written everything down, set it aside for a day or two. When you return to it, reread it carefully, challenging your points and especially your assumptions. If you still can't decide, try this exercise again. I know, I know: *bo-ring*. But the repetition and self-evaluation will pay off in helping you make a reasoned, intelligent, unbiased decision.

Finally, you're ready to get to work. You've identified all your constraints, decided on your specific goals. You've developed a plan. You've identified the resources and strategies you need to work around your constraints and accomplish the goals you've set.

What's next? Now it's time to begin gathering information. But how will you find the information you need? And what will you do with the information once you find it? These are substantial challenges in their own right, given all the information we have access to in today's world. To face these challenges, we need to throw everything we thought we knew about organization out the window. We need a radically new, twenty-first-century definition of *organization*—one that takes into account how our society and our brain really work. And we need a new set of tools that are appropriate for that definition and for the world we live in today. That's the focus of Part Two.

ENCODE THIS

- A clearly mapped out goal (and action plan to achieve it) gives context and purpose to everything you do and helps you organize your actions much more effectively.

- When you know your goals, it's easier to know what's important to do and not do, what information you need to keep in your brain, and what information you don't. This makes it easier to be efficient and organized.

- Being specific about your goals is essential. The more specific your goals are, the easier they are to achieve, and the easier your results are to measure.

- It also helps to be flexible about the outcome of your goals, so you'll be open to finding new ways to achieve them if your first approach fails.

- To determine your specific goals, ask yourself questions like: What is it I really need to achieve, above all else, and why do I need to achieve it? What will happen if I don't do it? What are the actions I have to take to make it happen?

- Once you know your goals and constraints related to an important project or task, set aside some time to clear your mind before getting to work. Then decide whether you should do the task you're considering at all, and whether you need to either delegate and/or ask for help.

- The bigger the plan, the bigger and more numerous your decisions are likely to be. Unfortunately, we're quite bad at making decisions. But we can learn to overcome, or at least compensate for, our poor decision-making skills. Some suggestions:

  ○ Bounce your decisions off someone whose opinion you trust. That person will help you spot any faulty logic or biases at work. Or he or she will reinforce that you've made a good decision.

  ○ Try the various outcomes of your decision on for size. "Live" with each decision for a little while, by visualizing its outcome to see how it feels.

  ○ Do your research. Additional information may help you make your decision. But don't overdo it. Too much information can actually make your decision harder.

  ○ Make a list of the pros and cons of the possible outcome of your decision. Try to prioritize them in order of importance.

  ○ Write down your entire arguments in favor of and opposed to the decision you're considering. After a day or two, reread what you've written and challenge your assumptions.

PRINCIPLES OF ORGANIZATION IN PART ONE

1. Organize your life to minimize brain strain.

2. Get stuff out of your head as quickly as possible.

3. Multitasking can actually make you less efficient.

4. Use stories to remember.

5. Just because something's always been done a certain way doesn't mean it *should* be.

6. Knowledge is not power. The *sharing* of knowledge is power.

7. Organize around actual constraints, not assumed ones.

8. Be completely honest—but never judgmental—with yourself.

9. Know when to ignore your constraints.

10. Know exactly where you're going—and how you'll get there—before you start the engine.

11. Be flexible about how you achieve your goals.

part two

THE NEW ORGANIZATION— AND HOW TO ACHIEVE IT

chapter 5

BEYOND TAYLORISM &
TRAPPER KEEPERS

why search matters

IN PART ONE, I challenged some commonly held assumptions about practically everything in the entire universe. There's one more I'd like to throw on the fire: that organization is the same, or should be, for everyone.

For years, this misconception has been at the heart of how we've learned and practiced organization skills. But when you think about it, the notion that organization is the same for everybody doesn't fly. No two people are the same; we all have our own individual differences, experiences, constraints, and foibles. In our far-flung and highly specialized world, our organizational needs aren't the same either. My needs for organization are bound to be different from yours, whether you're a CEO, a physicist, or a stay-at-home mom.

> I'm only human /
> Born to make
> mistakes.
>
> —Human League,
> "Human"

But again, I offer good news. With all the technological advances of the past few years, we don't *need* to all use the same strategies for organization. Today, there are tons of highly customizable tools to help us get organized—like Google's free Gmail, a cloud e-mail service that you can turn into your own personal, searchable information archive and that you can get to from any Internet-connected computer or phone. (I'll talk about Gmail at length in chapter 9.) We can use these tools to devise organizational systems that serve our individual needs today.

If the old one-size-fits-all notion of organization is outdated—and it is—what we need now is an entirely new approach to being organized. We need a new concept of organization that recognizes our individual differences, factors in our constraints and goals, and takes advantage of technology wherever possible. Organization in the twenty-first century, as I see it, even gives us the freedom to be—you read it here first—a bit disorganized.

Welcome to Part Two. It's all about the new conception of organization we need for today, which focuses on managing the information in our lives as well as the stress. While I encourage you to build your own organizational practices and systems, I suggest you begin with a tool you're probably already using multiple times a day: search. With so much knowledge available online, and so much information we have to keep track of, search has become as essential as oxygen.

Chapter 6 is about why search is the foundation of the new organization we need today, and how to master it. From there, the question becomes: Now that you've got this information, what do you do with it? In chapter 7, I'll share with you my techniques for getting stuff into my head. Then, in chapters 8, 9, 10, and 11, I'll show you how I get stuff *out* of my head. These chapters are about the tools—both paper and digital—I rely on to organize the thoughts, ideas, and information that buzz around me every day. My goal is not to have you use these same exact strategies but to have you learn from them and perhaps borrow from them to create a system that works for you.

Why Organization Isn't the Same for Everyone

You weren't born with a sense of organization; you had to learn it. And like everything else that's learned, it's learned in ways that are particular to us as individuals. It's like being taught how to swim. There are some general rules for how to do the backstroke or the butterfly. But mostly, you have to learn how to do the required motions your way. Your strokes won't be exactly the same as anyone else's because no one else shares your precise body shape and size or your specific muscle strength.

Likewise, organization isn't—nor should it be—exactly the same for everybody. Sure, there are fundamental guidelines to being organized that can apply to many people in many circumstances—things like to-do lists, carrying a small notebook at all times, putting everything in a certain place and remembering where that place is. But these things alone don't qualify as an organizational system.

In my humble opinion, the one-size-fits-all view of organization is a bit too Taylorist. It's fine if you're a machine or aspire to be one. But living, breathing beings need systems for organizing that take our humanness and differences into account. For example, as a dyslexic kid, I struggled to keep track of my school assignments, pencils, notes, and whatever else I was carrying around—things that came more easily to other kids. And it was more important for me to be organized than it was for my classmates because I needed every bit of brain power I could muster to focus on my schoolwork. Unfortunately, the traditional rules of organization didn't factor in my dyslexia, so I had to come up with my own.

In middle school, I started using a Trapper Keeper—which, as anyone who came of age in the eighties knows, is a three-ring binder with folders, tab dividers, and a Velcro flap enclosure. I kept my pencils and pens in a zippered, plastic pouch that attached to the rings inside the binder.

It worked. Consolidating my school stuff in one place, as the prevailing rules of organization dictated, helped me focus my mental capacity where it was needed most: my homework. I loved my Trapper Keeper—until one fateful day that turned me against such one-size-fits-all organization systems for good.

I was the classic eighty-pound, bespectacled geek (you know the type). In biology class, I sat next to a pretty blonde who was the love of my young life. One day, as I was putting my pencil into the Trapper Keeper's pouch, she looked over and started snickering. Then, to my horror, she turned to her friend and said, in a stage whisper, "He has one of those stupid pencil things!"

Love hurts.

—Nazareth, "Love Hurts"

Humiliated, I got rid of my Trapper Keeper and my "stupid pencil thing" immediately. The progress I'd been making toward being better organized was temporarily derailed. I knew then and there that the conventional systems for being organized weren't going to work for me. But I didn't give up easily, and as I grew up, I began to devise my own systems of organizing in general, and organizing information in particular, that worked for me. (I'll explain how I did this—by filtering information—in chapter 7.)

Predicting the Future

While our traditional methods for being organized don't accommodate our individual differences, they don't take into account the limitations of our brains either.

Consider filing cabinets. All the books on organization I read years ago talked about the importance of learning to file papers correctly. So I learned to file. It made sense, of course. If you didn't organize your receipts in some logical fashion, you'd have to dig through boxes or grocery bags at tax time to find what you needed. In fact, I still use filing cabinets today in some cases, as you'll see in chapter 8.

But the filing cabinet model doesn't take into account our brain's limitations, nor does it take advantage of new technological advances. To wit: Filing information in cabinets—and then finding that information again later—requires you to know exactly how you might use a document in the future

WHAT'S ALL THIS TALK ABOUT "THE CLOUD"?

Aside from a billowy white puffball in the sky, what exactly do people mean when they talk about "the cloud"?

Despite the recent popularity of terms like "the cloud" and "cloud computing," engineers have used clouds in their diagrams for many years. Originally, a cloud was used to designate a network whose inner workings were unknown to the person drawing the diagram or were largely irrelevant. And so, over time, the Internet was nicknamed "the cloud" and the name stuck.

Today, the term "cloud computing" generally refers to a huge range of services and software tools delivered in real time over the Internet, such as e-mail, calendar, contacts, and file backup/sharing/syncing services. Rather than storing information on a personal computer's drive or on a portable disk, you can use these services to store all information on the Internet ("in the cloud"), which means you can access your information and documents from any computer or other device connected to the Internet (like a phone with a Web browser). Your information sits in one place. You've got many ways to get to it. And you don't have to worry about losing data on your computer, should your hard drive fail or get infected with a virus.

If you can use a Web browser and have an Internet connection (usually through a DSL or cable service provider), you can use most cloud services. Among those I find extremely useful for organization are Google's free Gmail e-mail service and MobileMe, Apple's pay-service (more about both in chapter 9).

Not everyone is a cloud computing advocate, of course. Many people don't like the idea of having personal and private information floating around in the ether. Some worry that when another party has your data, you lose a certain amount of control over it. Others fret about security. Some hate the idea that all their online activities—purchases, e-mails, and so on—can be monitored and tracked by marketers. But for me, for reasons you'll soon read about, the advantages of cloud computing outweigh the concerns.

so you can label it appropriately. If you can't do that, you can't find that document when you need it.

For example, a few years back, you may have received a new travel policy memo at your company in your physical inbox. You would need to refer to that memo the next time you took a business trip, so you could fill out the expense report properly and therefore get reimbursed quickly. But what if your next business trip wasn't for another two months? Where should you file this particular interoffice memo in the interim?

Most of us would do the same thing at this point. Most likely, you'd have written something like "Expense report procedures" on the tab of a manila folder, filed the memo in the folder, and then filed the folder in the drawer dedicated to financial stuff. But how would you remember that your financial drawer was where you filed the travel memo?

Maybe you decided to store the memo in the three-ring binder human resources gave you, which explained (ad nauseam) all the company's rules and procedures. Same problem: Would you remember later that you filed the memo in the binder?

Perhaps, to compensate for the likelihood that you might forget where you filed the memo, you made three copies of it. You filed one in a folder in the "Financial stuff" drawer, another in the HR binder, and a third in a new folder that would contain travel information for your next trip. This strategy would likely work, although it would require you to perform the same filing task three times, and it would contribute to deforesting the Amazon.

Today, you're more likely to receive that memo as an e-mail. Great; you can forget about filing it. Just leave it in your e-mail inbox. Your inbox will eventually get as messy and unwieldy as your filing cabinets, of course. You won't have a clue where anything is, and you won't be able to see all your messages in one screen. But there's one fundamental difference between physical and electronic filing. In an e-mail inbox, you don't have to know where to look when you want to find something. That's where search comes in. When you need the information in the memo, just type a few keywords to search for it.

And that brings us to my twelfth principle of organization—one that's essential to the new organization we need now: *Don't file your information; search for it.*

Don't file your information; search for it.

That's the beauty of search. It doesn't matter in which file or folder you put that e-mail. In fact, I'd argue you don't need to put e-mail into folders at all and that you can use just a few high-level folders to organize all your computer files. A search on your computer will find the e-mail or file you need, probably in the time it would take you to roll your chair over to the filing cabinet. Even if a memo didn't arrive as an e-mail, you can scan it, keep the digital file on your computer or in the cloud, and search for it when you need it.

In other words: Search is what we need to survive and thrive in the information age. It's the foundation of the new organization. In the next chapter, I'll show you how to perform faster, more targeted searches so you can always find what you need, when you need it, *without* predicting the future (and it'll minimize the risk of paper cuts too).

ENCODE THIS

- Organization is *not* the same for everybody. The long-held notion that the same set of organizing methods would work for everyone doesn't take into account our individual differences, experiences, constraints, and foibles.

- With all the technological advances of the past few years, the old rules of being organized are outdated and don't serve our needs today.

- What we need now is an entirely new approach to being organized that recognizes our differences, takes our constraints and foibles into account, and leverages technology wherever possible. The new organization even gives us the freedom to be a bit disorganized.

- Search is the foundation of the new organization. We don't have to spend time and energy filing and hunting for critical information. All we have to do is search for it.

chapter 6

PARIS, FRANCE, OR PARIS, VEGAS?

how to master the art of search

MORE THAN ANY OTHER technology or innovation, search makes it possible for us to survive and thrive in the information age. Like oxygen, which changes everything it touches, the ability to quickly search computer files, e-mails, calendar entries, databases, and the Web has changed how we store information, how we retrieve it, how we use it. In other words, search has set us free from the clutter of our imperfect minds.

Thanks to search, you no longer have to neatly organize all your information the way you used to, with a place for everything and everything in its place. It's as if you no longer have to hang up all your clothes. Instead, you can just toss them into an ever-growing pile, and when you want to wear your favorite Nine Inch Nails T-shirt, just ask for it, and it will magically surface to the top of the heap. How freeing.

Over the past ten to fifteen years, computer-assisted search has become an integral part of our lives. It's evolved from something only academics and scientists could do on their monster computers into something most of us perform instinctively, multiple times daily. We breathe, we blink, we eat, we sleep, we Google.

As a result, most of us haven't paid much attention to search. In fact, by now we've pretty much taken it for granted. But search is actually a skill, one that's essential to the new organization. The savvier you become at search, the better you can filter out what's not important and focus on what is. The ability to perform quick, targeted searches helps you find the information you need faster. And you don't have to expend mental capacity trying to anticipate where to look for a piece of information or trying to figure out where the heck to put it. You just search for what you want, and *voilà*.

> **Whoomp! There it is.**
>
> —Tag Team, "Whoomp! There It Is"

So let's work on mastering search. In this chapter, I'll share some strategies and tips for getting the best results from your queries. My focus here is on Google because the majority of people use it.[1] And despite its many competitors, I believe Google, with its streamlined search interface and sophisticated algorithms for delivering the most relevant results, continues to offer the best search engine. (Okay, it doesn't hurt that I used to work there either.) For ideas about other search engines, see the "Stuff We Love" appendix. That's where you'll find a brief guide to the tools and services I'll talk about in Part Two, along with suggestions for alternatives.

Crawling the Web

Google and most search engines use automated software agents called *crawlers*, also known as *spiders* or *robots*. Crawlers visit Web sites frequently, reading and capturing most of a page's text as well as following links to other pages within the site.

The information about a site the crawler collects is added to the search engine's index of Web pages. When you perform a query, the search engine rapidly analyzes the information in its index to find matches. The results of your search are listed in order of relevance, with the most relevant pages listed first. (I'm talking, of course, about *organic* search results, not the paid results, which are small, text-only advertisements you see at the very top and on the right side of Google search results pages.)

The search engine determines what's most relevant to your query using many different factors. Google uses over 200 factors, including where on the page your search term appears and how often the term appears. For example, I just did a search on the word *videoconferencing*, and Google found millions of pages (as of this moment in time, 2,020,000, to be exact). Among the top search results at that time were a Wikipedia entry and a *BusinessWeek* article. In both cases, the word *videoconferencing* appeared in the Web page's title (that's where location comes in). And the word showed up at least four times in the entry and article (that's the frequency factor at work).

While most search engines follow this general model, no two search engines do things exactly the same. That explains why you can get different results using the same term on different search engines.

Google's PageRank[2] algorithm is one of the ways Google differs from other search engines. When Google's cofounders Larry Page and Sergey Brin met, they were both graduate students in computer science at Stanford University. They had a class project to come up with a way to find valuable information within piles of data. This project led to the development of PageRank.

PageRank judges the likelihood that a particular Web page is "good" in the same way we tend to judge other people. For example, if you ran into a stranger on the street and, for some odd reason, he started to explain search to you, you probably wouldn't take him seriously. Why should you? He's a stranger. You have no way of knowing if what he says is legitimate.

However, you bought this book, and you're reading this chapter. Quite possibly, you believe I have something useful to say about search. Why are you inclined to believe me, and not the stranger on the street? Mostly, it's because the publisher wouldn't have let me write this book if I didn't know what I was talking about. (Right?) In other words, you believe me because someone you trust (the publisher) trusts me.

PageRank essentially works in the same manner. Instead of asking people it trusts, PageRank looks to see if Web pages link to the page it's ranking. It "trusts" a Web page more when plenty of contextually relevant pages on other sites link to it. In other words, if lots of relevent pages link to a page, that page for some reason must be worthy of all those links. Thus, that page is probably "good." And, as such, it receives a higher PageRank, which helps move it up in Google search results.

By the way, you might assume that PageRank got its name because it ranks Web pages. But you'd be wrong. In a pun, Larry Page named it after himself.

Ranking search results accurately is difficult to do, primarily because there's a lot of complexity in our language. For example, if I told you only that I went to the bank, would you know for certain that I went to a place to get money? Or would you think I'd been hanging out by the side of a river?

Similarly, if you did a search for *apples,* how would the search engine know if you were looking for results related to a fruit or for a particular technology company? Google algorithms make an educated guess based on enormous amounts of data compiled from millions and millions of past searches. In this case, Google guesses that usually, if you type *apples* as a search word, you're probably searching for information about the fruit. Google hedges its bets a bit; the top search results you're likely to get will be for the fruit as well as for the technology company. However, if you enter *apple,* the odds increase markedly that you're looking for the technology company. In this case, your top search results are overwhelmingly related to Apple the company. Thus, Google gives different rankings of results depending on whether the *s* is there or not. For other searches, it can get even more complicated. That's why Google and its competitors employ hundreds of engineers to constantly tune their engines to deliver the most relevant results.

Getting the Most Relevant Search Results

Okay, we've peeked under the hood to see how the engine works. Now let's get behind the wheel and explore how to get the most from a Google search.

Google searches are quick and easy, and they usually deliver the results you're looking for. But sometimes, the results are too broad for what you need and you end up with page after page of results it would take hours to sift through. If that happens, there are ways to tweak your standard Google search to get better results. Here are a few:

Be as descriptive as possible. If you simply type *apple*, as in the earlier example, you'll get hundreds of millions of search results. But if what you're really searching for is information about engraving an Apple iPod Touch, you should use a search phrase like *apple ipod touch engrave*. Your search results will be much more targeted to your interests. (I've italicized search terms in this chapter just to set them apart; you don't need to italicize search phrases.)

Use quotation marks around a phrase. When you add quotes around two or more words, Google (and other search engines) will give you only those pages with that exact phrase. For example, let's pretend you're heading to Paris this summer for vacation (lucky *vous*) and you want to research hotels. If you simply search for the words *Paris hotels*, Google will look for pages relating to hotels with the two words used somewhere in relatively close proximity to one another on the page. Google will usually assume you're searching for those words together as a phrase, but it's just guessing. As a result, you may find a link to the Paris Hotel in Las Vegas among the many pages of search results. Not exactly what you are looking for. On the other hand, using quotation marks around the two words will confine your search results to Web pages where the two words *"Paris hotels"* are used as a phrase, thus excluding this somewhat less exotic (though I suppose that's debatable) vacation destination in the desert. (Searches on

Google and other engines don't have to be case sensitive. So it's okay to type *paris* instead of *Paris*.)

Search for adjectives. You don't want to get information about just any Paris hotel; after all, you're on a budget. You could narrow your results by including the words *affordable*, *cheap*, and *budget* in your search. And try using various synonyms—you might think it's great if a hotel is *cheap*, but its marketing team probably prefers to bill it as *affordable*. There are several ways you could do this in Google.

Type this search string *"paris hotels" ~affordable* in Google (this trick doesn't usually work in other search engines). Placing the tilde symbol (~) immediately before a word tells Google to look for Web pages containing the word (in this case, *affordable*) and others like it (such as *cheap*, *budget*, and other synonyms). Be careful *not* to put a space between the tilde symbol and the word you want to search for.

Alternatively, you could type this: *"paris hotels" affordable OR cheap OR budget*. Your search results will include pages containing the phrase *Paris hotels* and at least one of the words *affordable*, *cheap*, or *budget*. By the way, *OR* when used in all caps is a standard search operator, so it should work with most search engines.

What's the difference between using the tilde symbol and *OR*? The tilde symbol is a wild card, giving Google carte blanche to find all the pages it thinks have words similar to *affordable*. In contrast, using *OR* will give you fewer search results because you're telling Google to look for pages containing only the words *affordable*, *cheap*, or *budget*. Bottom line: If you're trying to narrow your results, use *OR* so you can specify the synonyms you want.

> I got a Nikon camera / I love to take a photograph.
>
> —Paul Simon, "Kodachrome"

Exclude what you don't want. You want to buy a digital camera to take on your Paris excursion, but for whatever reason, you don't like Nikons. (I'm not knocking Nikon; I just needed an example here.) Here's what you'd type in Google (and in most other search engines): *digital camera -Nikon* (or to be even more precise, *"digital camera" -Nikon*).

The minus symbol, placed immediately before the word *Nikon* with no space between them, tells Google to search for pages about digital cameras from all manufacturers other than Nikon.

Here's another way the minus sign is useful in a search. Imagine that you're trying to find general information about opera, as in "O Sole Mio," and not Opera, the Web browser. In your Google search, you'd type *opera –browser*. Your results will exclude the Web browser.

Get specific with numeric ranges. On Google, an ellipsis (three consecutive periods) can be used to express a range of numbers. So if you want to specify exactly how affordable that digital camera should be, you could type this in Google: *"digital camera" $100…$300*. That will tell Google to narrow its results to digital cameras costing between $100 and $300. (This trick doesn't always work in other search engines.)

Search a particular site. While most Web sites offer tools for searching their own pages, these tools are sometimes suboptimal. What many people don't know is that you can use Google to search the content of a specific Web site. Because its algorithms are more sophisticated than the search tools used by some Web sites, you'll usually get better results using Google (though more and more sites are using Google-powered search these days). The command for this is *site:* with no space after the colon, followed by the URL of the site you want to search. For example, are you curious about what the *New York Times* has published about Paris hotels? You could go to the *Times*'s Web site and type *"Paris hotels"* in its search box. Or, better yet, you could run this standard Google search: *"paris hotels" site:nytimes.com*. (This works with most other search engines too.)

Look for a particular file type. Now you've got to figure out how you'll pay for that trip to Paris. There's bound to be an Excel spreadsheet somewhere on the Web that will help you create a budget, right? You could find it by Googling this phrase: *"personal budget" filetype:xls*. Using *filetype:xls* tells Google (and most other search engines) to look for Excel spreadsheets relating to personal budgets. (Excel's file format is xls.) Among the other types of files you can easily search for using this method are PDF documents (pdf), Word files (doc), and PowerPoint presentations (ppt).

These simple search commands take seconds to use, yet can save you an incredible amount of time and effort when it comes to narrowing your results. They're pretty amazing, when you think about it—and yet the average Web surfer doesn't know about them.

Your Search Engine Is Also a Calculator

Google isn't just for finding Web pages. Let's say there's a particular fact or statistic you need to find, and fast. Not to worry, Google can help. Here are some ways I use Google to quickly look up all kinds of facts. (Most of these tricks work in Yahoo! Search and Microsoft's Bing, among others.)

Currency conversions. A standard Google search such as *100 euros in dollars* will convert one currency into another. It works the other way too; you can do a search on *euros in USD*, to convert euros into U.S. dollars (or pesos, or yen, for that matter).

Measurement conversions. This is incredibly useful if, like me, you can't seem to get a handle on that crazy metric system. Google converts liquid, distance, and other measures. Example: the search phrase *1 mile in km* converts 1 mile into kilometers; *pound in ounces* reveals how many ounces are in a pound; *inch in mm* tells you how many millimeters are in an inch; and so on. As with the currency conversions, the word *in* signals to Google you want to convert from one system of measurement to another.

Time. Typing *time Paris* will give you the current time in that city. No math required.

Weather. Want to know the current temperature in Paris? Type *weather paris*.

Maps. To see an address on a Google map, just type the street address and city in Google.

Flight status. Find out if your spouse's flight will be on time by entering the airline and flight number, such as *American Airlines 123*. That's *without* the annoying pop-up ads or the soul-sucking hold music.

Foreign-language translations. Ever wondered how to translate essential travel phrases, such as *"How much is that purple shirt?"* from English into French? (Or Spanish, Dutch, or Ukrainian?) Google Translate (translate.google.com) will translate words, sentences, and chunks of text from one language to another. You tell it which languages you're converting from and to, and within a few seconds, you've got the translation. Yahoo! also offers a good translation tool, BabelFish (babelfish.yahoo.com).

Definitions. Don't know exactly what *discombobulated* means? (Unfortunately, I know all too well.) If you type just the word *discombobulated*, that's exactly what the search results will be. Instead, do a search on *define discombobulated* or any other word whose meaning eludes you.

Phone numbers. Plagued by prank callers? Stalkers? Creditors? When a phone number you don't recognize pops up on your caller ID, try this search: *phonebook: 212-555-1212* (substituting the number you're looking up). Or, to look up someone's phone number, try this: *phonebook: John Smith Anywhere NY.*

Stock quotes. Type a company's stock symbol, such as *AAPL* for Apple, to get the current stock quote. If you don't know what Apple's symbol is, you can simply enter *Apple stock* and you'll get both the symbol and the latest stock price. (This trick works for looking up many, but not all, company stock exchange symbols.)

Shipment status. Expecting a package from FedEx, UPS, or some other shipper? Typing the tracking number into Google will give you an update on the package's current status, without your having to navigate to the carrier's Web site.

Calculations. The Google standard search box is also a calculator in disguise. Some examples:

Use the standard calculator symbols: * for *multiplied by*, / for *divided by*, and so on.

Math geeks can type complex equations such as *5*9+(sqrt 10)^3=*, and Google will provide the answer, which, in case you're wondering, is 76.6227766.

Spell checker. Not sure how to spell a word? Type what you think is correct into Google. In most cases, it will suggest the correct spelling or it will search for pages containing the word or phrase properly spelled. However, here you should be careful because Google won't always know what you mean by your misspelled word. For example, if you weren't sure how to spell the word *mettle*, as in "testing your mettle," and you typed *mettal* into Google, you may get a bunch of search results for Mattel, the toy company.

Movie show times. A Google search for a movie's name and your Zip code, such as *Spider-Man 94114*, will give you theater locations and show times in your hood.

This is what I'm talking about when I say that today, there's no longer any need to store all this minutiae in our brains (not that we could if we wanted to, anyway). The Google brain is storing it for us—and that brain never gets taxed, tired, or overwhelmed by stress.

You don't even have to be at your computer to take advantage of these tricks—they'll work with Google on your mobile phone's Web browser. In fact, your phone doesn't even need a browser or an Internet connection. You can look up all sorts of basic information just by sending a text message to Google at 466453. For instance, you could get the phone number of a business by texting the name and city (such as *Drake Hotel Chicago*) to Google. Within a few seconds, you'll get the information you want sent to your phone in a text message. And you'll have saved yourself the time and cost of making a directory assistance call.

Speaking of directory assistance, Google also offers another free service. If you dial 800-466-4411, Google will look up a business by name, city, and state, and then automatically connect you.

The Small Stuff

I've got a few more tips to keep in mind as you Google:

- You don't need to type most common words and characters, such as *a, and, how, where,* and *the* into a search engine query. Typically, Google and other search engines don't need those words to figure out what you're trying to find. If a common word is essential to your search, however, the best approach is to include the entire phrase in quotation marks. For example, my coauthor writes under the byline James A. Martin. If you simply Googled *james a martin,* you'd also get results for James H. Martin, James C. Martin, and so on. Putting quotes around *"james a martin"* limits the results to that particular name.

- Google automatically searches for pages containing common variations of a keyword. For example, a search using the word *exercise* would also look for relevant instances of the words *exercises, exercised,* and *exercising.*

Searching Your Computer

Search wouldn't be so freeing if it only applied to information on the Web. Fortunately, search also works on your computer, liberating you from having to store files and e-mail in folders in order to organize them.

You can search the entire contents of your computer using the free Google Desktop utility (desktop.google.com) for

Windows, Mac, and Linux computers. Or you can use the search tools that are part of the Windows and Macintosh operating systems. Using these tools, you don't have to set up lots of file folders on your hard drive, then drag and drop files into them. You can be as disorganized as you want and search for files when they're needed. You can perform desktop searches quickly too. In some cases, you start receiving search results before you even finish typing your query.

Google Desktop and your computer's operating system search tools work in a fairly similar fashion. Each indexes lots of different types of files stored on your computer, as well as on any drives (such as a backup hard drive) attached to it. The index, similar to the index that Google and other search engines create, contains the text information that's inside your documents. However, the more files you have, the slower your desktop indexing can be. (Sometimes, when speed is superimportant to me, I turn Google Desktop's indexing off.)

Desktop search tools index and then search across all sorts of files stored anywhere on your hard drive (not just on your computer desktop). The types of files indexed and searched can include e-mail, Word documents, Excel spreadsheets, PDFs, PowerPoint presentations, contacts, calendar appointments, and Web browser bookmarks. Text associated with images, videos, and music files, such as their file names, are also included. Desktop search tools vary a bit in terms of which file types they index and search, but most will search all those I've listed.

It's pretty easy to start a desktop search. For example, in Windows Vista, launch the Start menu, then just start typing your search word or phrase in the "Start Search" field at the bottom of the menu. On a Mac, find the magnifying glass icon (it's always on the top right of the screen), click it, and start typing.

In many cases, the same search shortcuts you've learned from your search engine queries will work in a computer search. For example, putting quotation marks around two or more words like *"Paris hotels"* in a desktop or Web search ensures that you get only the results in which those words appear together, rather than the results that simply contain both words.

Thanks to desktop search, I don't organize computer files by putting them into folders within folders within folders. In most cases, I simply save a file in the main Documents folder. Or if I have a lot of files related to a specific topic, as I did with this book, I'll gather them into their own folder. The beauty of search is that it allows you to keep your documents in as few, or as many, folders as you want.

Relying on search to organize information on your computer may seem risky to you, at least in the beginning. Maybe you don't quite trust search to find what you're looking for. Or it could be your brain is simply used to putting computer files into folders within folders, and anything else feels foreign. If that's the way you prefer to do it, that's okay too. As I've said before, my way of being organized might not be right for you, and vice versa. The point is to show you that you don't *have* to do things a certain way just because that's how you've always done them; to help you open yourself up to trying new ways of organizing; and to show you how to make the most out of the tools available—should you choose to use them.

> Now it's clear / And I know what I have to do.
>
> —Iron Maiden, "Still Life"

Of course, finding the information you need is only the beginning. To truly be organized, you have to decide what to do with that information once you've found it. Should you encode it? Store it for later use? Ignore it completely? In the next chapter, I'll show you how I encode information I need to be organized using two techniques: *filtering* and *repetition*.

ENCODE THIS

- Because of search, you no longer have to neatly organize all your information the way you would with physical files, with a place for everything and everything in its place.

- Search is the foundation of the organizational systems we need today. These systems weren't possible even five years ago because we didn't have until recently the digital tools these systems required.

- It's important we learn how to master search because it has become an essential part of our everyday lives.

- The savvier you become at search, the better and faster you can filter out what's not important—so you can focus on what is.

- No two search engines do things exactly the same. That's why you can get varying results using the same term on different search engines.

- There are lots of easy ways to refine Google searches to get the best results. Learning these tricks will save you time and energy and, most importantly, deliver the information you need.

chapter 7

COLORED MARKERS & FILTERS

making information stick

NOT LONG AGO, at least in geologic time, only the chosen few could publish their thoughts, writings, or any other form of creative expression. Even for the rich, the powerful, the wildly talented, however, there were no assurances. Media companies and producers weren't usually interested in anything that wasn't likely to sell lots of copies or tickets. After all, they have to make a living too.

But in recent years, something truly extraordinary has happened. Anyone with Internet access can now publish his or her stories, articles, videos, photos, and philosophical musings for a global audience with few if any barriers, and at little or no cost. The result: The Internet has evolved into an ever-expanding universe of human experience and knowledge. And while this democratization of information has given us a far richer understanding of our world, there's just one little problem.

On any given day, an enormous amount of content begs for our attention: e-mail, text messages, instant messages, blogs, Twitter tweets, Web sites, wikis, Flickr photos, Facebook and LinkedIn updates, Yelp reviews, podcasts, video podcasts, YouTube videos, and more. That's in addition, of course, to all the books, newspapers, magazines, radio programs, movies, TV shows, and other forms of mass media we routinely consume. In many ways, it's great that we have all this information at our fingertips. But how do we absorb any of it?

While the amount of information seems infinite, the time and mental capacity we have to take it all in certainly isn't. None of us, no matter how good our memories might be, can possibly store even a fraction of this incoming information in our heads. I know that if I tried, pretty soon, my brain would be spewing smoke like an overheated car engine.

Luckily, the vast majority of information we receive doesn't need to be encoded. Indeed, most facts aren't worth remembering. For example, unless I'm studying for a geology exam, why on Earth would I need to remember the difference between stalactites and stalagmites? If I ever found myself in need of that fact, I'd just look it up using Wikipedia or Google. With all the information available online today, and with the ubiquity of wireless Internet and Internet-enabled mobile devices like the iPhone, no matter where I am, I can ask practically any question of the universe and get an answer.

> Here we are now / Entertain us.
>
> —Nirvana, "Smells Like Teen Spirit"

That said, it's not really efficient, or even possible, to go through life Googling every piece of information we need, every time we need it. And while we certainly don't need to keep every bit of information in our heads, we do need convenient access to the information we need to do our jobs, conduct our daily lives, and be organized. For all the information that's specific to our world but doesn't need to be kept in our brains, it's critical to have some sort of organizational system in place.

I'll give you an example. Let's say you and I met, and you gave me your business card. I'm sure you're a nice person, but why should I bother memorizing your phone number? It would simply be unnecessarily taking up space in my already overloaded brain. What's more, no offense, but even if I did try to encode your number, without a context or a story for it, I'm probably not going to remember it anyway, so I'm not even going to try. Just because I'm not going to memorize it, however, doesn't mean I don't want to hang on to it so that it's available when I need it. I'll simply store your number with all the others I keep on my computer and my iPhone. Those tools do a much better job than I can of remembering, and at least one of them is always close at hand.

Ultimately, the challenge we face is this: With all sorts of information coming at us every day, how do we know what to ignore, what to store electronically or on paper for later use, and what to encode in our memory? And that's only the first step. Once we've identified what we need to keep on hand, how do we know what's the best system for storing and organizing it? And when it comes to the information we need to keep in our heads, how can we help ourselves encode it successfully? That's the focus of this chapter.

Your Goals Are Your Guide

Every day, you take in new information through reading, observing, talking to others, and so on. But how do you know what to do with each piece of information as it's received? Usually, your goals, which, as I've mentioned, should be based your needs and interests, will guide you. If a piece of information isn't relevant to your goals, your brain will likely automatically ignore it. The fact will enter and exit your short-term memory at lightning speed.

When information you come across *does* relate to a goal, your brain will most likely take note. Once you've determined the information is important, then it's time to decide if you should hold on to the information by storing it digitally or on paper, and/or by encoding it (moving it from short-term memory into long-term memory).

Imagine that you're casually reading the news online. One article you see quotes a statistic showing that Macintosh computers are gaining popularity among business users. You work in the computer industry, and the statistic might be useful to you later. But you're not sure *how* it might be useful or when, because at the moment, you don't have any goals or context for that information. Your next step might be to bookmark the Web page where the article appears. Or you could copy and paste the article into an e-mail and send it to yourself, where it becomes part of your searchable e-mail archive (more about using your e-mail as a personal database in chapter 9).

On the other hand, if you came across that statistic and you're interviewing for a marketing job at Apple next week, your goals for that information are clear. You need to encode it, so you can bring it up during the job interview and show you've done your homework.

Unfortunately, encoding, as I explained in chapter 1, requires effort—especially if you're trying to encode a lot of information at one time. If you don't rehearse information, you risk dropping it out of short-term memory. And if you rehearse a piece of information sloppily, you risk remembering it incorrectly. For these reasons, you have to be picky about what you try to remember, and how you try to remember it. That's why I rely on organization principle no. 13: *Only keep in your head what truly needs to be there.*

> **Only keep in your head what truly needs to be there.**

How do you do that? By *filtering*.

Filtering Out What You Don't Need

Filtering is a technique that helps me avoid encoding information I don't need. When I filter, I isolate information I believe is important according to my goals for that information. Everything else, I ignore.

Before we can encode a piece of information, we usually first have to read it. But my dyslexia makes reading difficult for me, so I've learned to develop systems that allow me to do the least amount of reading possible. For example, as a student, when I was faced with sifting through enormous amounts of information on a daily basis, I came up with a system for filtering out what I didn't need to encode, so I didn't waste time and effort on reading unimportant stuff. At the time, it was simply a survival strategy to get me through my classes. But it proved to be so useful in other areas that, over time, it became the cornerstone of my organizational efforts. In fact, my system helped prepare me for the challenge of dealing with too much information, something many of us face today.

Here's how it worked: When I sat down to read, I'd line up four colored highlighters and a pen in some bright color, say, purple. As I skimmed the pages, I'd look for things that seemed important to the goals I had for the information.

When I found something of interest, I'd place a star next to it in the margins using my colored-ink pen. I didn't try to relate the pieces I'd starred to anything else at this point. I just marked what appeared to be significant, which had the effect of filtering out everything else.

Once I finished going through a chapter, I'd reread only those sentences or sections I'd starred with my colored pen. During this second pass-through, I'd assign each starred item to one of four simple categories, depending on my goal for that piece of information. Then I'd give each category its own color. For example, when I read a chapter in a math text-book, I used the following categories and colors:

- I marked definitions of new terms and concepts (the goal being to memorize them) with a yellow highlighter.

- I marked math equations and derivations with pink (to figure out the patterns).

- I highlighted things I didn't understand with blue (so I could go back to them and reread them more carefully later).

- I marked solutions to sample problems with green (the goal being to check them against my own answers).

By color-coding information into categories, I broke down an overwhelming monolith of seemingly unrelated words into small, related pieces. This made the task a hundred times more manageable. It was the difference between trying to build something out of a mile-high pile of lumber and assembling something out of a set of Lego blocks.

> **I see your true colors shining through.**
>
> —Cyndi Lauper, "True Colors"

Then, skimming the chapter the third time, I could easily spot the highlighted passages. I could read them again more carefully, trying to determine what each one meant and how it related to the other highlighted parts. This would help me see patterns and develop a story about the *important* information in the chapter, which in turn gave it context and thus, made the information easier to encode. Thanks to this technique, I became a world-class speed reader, a skill that's been invaluable to me ever since.

My system was amazingly efficient. Reading—the hardest part of studying for me—was reduced to skimming. As I zipped through textbook pages, I spotted key themes and rules to remember. I filtered out most everything else, to avoid cluttering my brain with unnecessary stuff.

> **I drew a line for you / And it was all yellow.**
>
> —Coldplay, "Yellow"

For the information I needed to memorize, I broke down the most important part of reading—understanding the information in the text—into bite-sized chunks I could digest one at a time.

Remember, the human brain is far better at remembering a lot of small chunks of information than at remembering a few big ones. And that brings me to my organization principle no. 14: *Break big chunks into small ones*, which applies to activities as well as to information. When you feel overwhelmed by something, it helps to break it down into smaller pieces and tackle each piece individually. My principle isn't groundbreaking, of course. Most if not all organization and efficiency experts advocate the same thing. But it's a helpful guideline for organizing the information we receive every day.

> **Break big chunks into small ones.**

To put my principle into action, try getting into the habit of identifying information in one of two ways: stuff you can ignore and information you might later need. Then break the second category into two groups: what you can physically store (on paper or electronically) for retrieving later and what you need to commit to memory. To help yourself encode information, try to put it into context by developing a story around it or attaching a goal to it.

Thanks to this system, I was fairly successful in my college courses. In fact, many of my classmates might even have described me as "smart." Some people appear smart because they can remember a string of unrelated facts. Others, because they can link facts together in a way that helps them uncover larger truths. And then there are those who can connect a set of facts in a unique way that offers fresh insights and perspectives. Whether I was smart or not isn't the point. My filtering technique was smart because it helped me overcome my brain's inherent limitations (and the additional ones imposed by my dyslexia) and organize information in a way that was most efficient and effective for me.

By now you might be thinking, well, that's great, but I'm not a student and I haven't cracked open a textbook in years. So how is this technique going to help me? Glad you asked. You see, later on in life, when I no longer needed to memorize mathematical terms or equations, I came up with similar methods to filter information in books, articles, and even e-mail.

For example, I use labels in Gmail to automatically filter as much of my incoming e-mail as possible. If I didn't filter my e-mail, I'd be perpetually overwhelmed by all the messages flooding my inbox. I wouldn't know where to start. I'll explain more about labels and filters in Gmail, and how I use them, in chapter 9.

I put my filtering technique to work in writing this book too, though in ways that are a bit different from how I filtered in college.

After Jim and I had written a chunk of chapters, we'd submit each chapter in its own Word file to our editor, Talia Krohn, for feedback. Talia then used Word's Comments tool to insert her editorial suggestions and questions throughout each chapter file.

I'd print the files Talia returned to us with both the original text and her comments displayed on each page. Next, as I skimmed the comments for the first time, I'd try to determine how to organize them into categories. My goal was to categorize the comments by priority—which ones would require the most effort, and which ones the least. This would enable me to more efficiently allocate my time and brain capacity when making revisions. For example, I could work on the easier revisions at the end of the day, when I was tired, and save the more challenging ones for times when I was more energetic and alert.

Once I'd finished the first read, I determined four categories of comments and assigned three of them a color. Here, my goal was to filter comments by task and difficulty level, rather than to filter based on the need to encode or learn, as I did when reading college textbooks.

Category 1 was minor stuff, such as a suggested rewording of a sentence. Typically, these were obvious fixes and weren't worth spending time evaluating. Since there were a fair amount of these comments in our early drafts, I decided not to mark them with a colored highlighter. If I had, whatever color I used would have dominated many of the pages, making it difficult for me to quickly scan for other highlighted sections.

Category 2 was for reorganized paragraphs or sections. These edits would require a little more thought than category 1 but usually would not require any action from Jim or me. I highlighted these comments in yellow because it's a soft color that blends in. Since these comments weren't the highest priority, they didn't need to leap off the pages at me as much as the category 3 and 4 comments.

Category 3 was for Talia's questions about a specific point or anecdote. These comments were of higher priority than category 1 and 2 because they would require more thought or effort on our part to address. So I highlighted category 3 comments prominently with a green marker.

Category 4 was for suggestions of things to add, like more examples to further drive home our points. Sometimes, this would require us to do additional research or thinking. Whatever the case, a category 4 comment meant Jim and I would need to add new text, which, like category 3, is more difficult to do than to make the edits suggested in category 1 and 2 comments.

By the way, this is another example of why it's important to have diverse perspectives on any project. As collaborators, Jim and I would sometimes fall into groupthink. We needed the help of an impartial, smart outsider—Talia, in this case—to show us areas of improvement we hadn't noticed on our own.

I use these methods of filtering and grouping information in my business life too. For example, I take notes in all the meetings I attend. But often these notes end up disorganized and confusing because the conversational threads in group discussions are often all over the map. We may start with topic A, then veer into topics B and C before returning to A. Some participants may interject non sequiturs that derail the discussion, while others may reach differing conclusions from the same information presented, sending the conversation off on tangents.

This isn't necessarily a bad thing; after all, meetings are the appropriate environment for people to voice new and divergent ideas. But the problem for me is that inevitably, the meeting notes I take reflect the often disorderly progression of information and conflicting views, making it hard to extract the information I need. So each week, I allocate time to rereading all my notes from that week's meetings. Often, I also use the filtering tricks I developed during my college days, highlighting and grouping information bits and moving related pieces of information together in a text file. (I type most of my meeting notes now on a laptop, which makes moving things around much easier, thanks to good old cut and paste—more about that in chapter 11.) The rereading and reordering help me to filter out the things that were said that weren't important and to remember the things that were.

The Rewards of Repetition

My filtering system has another advantage. It makes it easy to quickly refer to key information, even if it's days or years after I first read it. This is particularly important for reasons discussed earlier: The human memory is incredibly fallible, and even when we encode information carefully, that doesn't necessarily guarantee it'll stay in long-term memory. When I need to refresh my memory about something, I can simply skim the color-highlighted material, instead of having to reread the entire thing.

Back in college, I didn't stop at just rereading my filtered notes, however. Often, I'd rewrite them by typing them into a text file on my computer as well. Then I'd cut and paste pieces of related information so they were physically next to one another. This process of grouping the information physically into categories, though a bit tedious, helped me to more easily develop some context to my notes. Here again, the repetition alone—of rereading and then rewriting the information—made it easier to encode what was important.

You go back, Jack / Do it again.

—Steely Dan, "Do It Again"

On the surface, repetition may not seem like a terribly sensible organization principle. After all, isn't it more efficient to do something once and do it well, rather than to repeat it several times? Although that's often true, repetition has its rewards, particularly when it comes to getting information into your head. Remember that repeating (or rehearsing) the information, either through writing it down or rereading it, clearly enhances recall. And when you can recall information you need, when you need it, you'll be more organized and successful.

So at the risk of repeating myself, let me introduce my fifteenth principle of organization: *Dedicate time each week to reviewing key information.* Practically every day, I receive or gather information that's relevant to my goals—whether it's meeting notes, e-mail, or PowerPoint presentations—and I set aside the information with the intent of rereading it when I'm not busy or distracted. For instance, if I'm reading a print-out of a computer file, I'll use colored markers or sticky notes to mark information I'll need to reread later. If it's an e-mail in Gmail, I star it; people who use Microsoft Outlook can flag messages for follow-up. If it's something I've read on my Amazon Kindle e-book reader, I'll use the Kindle tool to mark the text and add it to my clippings. And if it's something I've read online, I'll bookmark the page.

> **Dedicate time each week to reviewing key information.**

Ultimately, if a piece of information seems complicated or not useful to memorize, I try to capture it in digital form. In digital form, information is easy to search, share, and access from my iPhone or any of the computers I regularly use (more about this in the following chapters).

Ideally, you should try to store all your various scraps of digital information you accumulate in one place. I recommend using your e-mail program for this purpose, especially if, like Gmail, it offers good search capabilities and you can access your entire history of messages from your computer and your phone.

For example, let's say you're extremely concerned about the environment. One day, you happen upon a travel article online about the Proximity Hotel in Greensboro, North Carolina, which is said to be one of the greenest hotels in the United States. You may never make it to that particular southern city. But if you do, or if someone you know later

Many kids today are nearly as busy as their parents; the only difference is, they're having way more fun. But even so, a busy schedule means there may be less time for homework (not to mention sleep). So how can you help your kids make the most of their study time? Here are a few suggestions:

Use stories. Stories, as I've mentioned, are a particularly useful way to remember facts. And any school-age kid understands the concept of stories. So if there are facts your kids (or teenagers) need to remember for school, help them build a story around each fact, or set of facts, no matter how tiny.

Use repetition. Once they've developed one or more stories, get your kids to retell them. Remember, repetition enhances recall, and repeating the information a few times will help them encode and remember the facts the stories are built around.

Prioritize. Ask your kids to identify the most important elements of what they're trying to learn, and then encourage them to focus on learning those elements first. This helps them prioritize their studying, which is important because kids, like adults, have a finite capacity for encoding. Plus, this helps introduce them to the practice of filtering.

Identify their limits. We've all got limits on how long we can concentrate, and when one hits those limits, performance drops markedly (yes, that means that all-night cramming sessions aren't useful). My ability to focus on something tends to vaporize after about ninety minutes. And these days, thanks to video games, the Internet, text messaging, and so on, kids can easily get distracted, and there's only so much a can of Red Bull can do. Try to help your kids recognize their study limits. Don't push them past those limits because instead of learning more, they'll just burn out—which pretty much ensures that they won't do well on

> the test. Instead, when they reach their limits, encourage
> them to take a brain break, to do something that relaxes
> and recharges them. Then, when they hit the books again,
> they're more likely to successfully encode what they need.

mentions she's going there, you'd want to know a good place to stay. So instead of clipping it and putting it in some file (which I guarantee you'll promptly forget doing), or bookmarking it on your browser, you copy and paste the text of that article about the hotel into an e-mail message. You might add a few extra keywords to the message too, such as *travel article green hotel greensboro north carolina*, and then send that message to yourself. Cool; now it's part of your searchable personal database. If you do this with all the various bits of information you want to keep, you'll never have to bother with trying to remember where you put it—you'll know it's always in Gmail (or whatever e-mail system you use).

Regardless of how you gather your information, rereading it when there's time to focus on it helps you determine what's not important and remember what is. If you can regularly set aside time every week to do this, you'll increase your chances of remembering information when you need it—and, thus, of becoming better organized.

Where Filtering Falls Down

Alas, my system of filtering isn't perfect.

By isolating bits of information and ignoring others, we can miss information that may in fact be important (we just don't realize it at the time). We also risk losing the isolated information's original meaning or context and developing erroneous inferences. This risk is particularly high when we don't know our goals for the information we're filtering.

Let's say I'm skimming through a collection of articles, looking for information to include in a presentation I'm preparing, but I haven't quite figured out exactly what I want to get across in the presentation. This makes it difficult to figure out what information I can ignore, what I should keep to put in the presentation, and what I should commit to memory in case someone asks a question about it. By filtering, I risk missing a piece of information that could prove to be important or useful or even forgetting a data point because I've filtered out some of its context.

But look at it this way: Because of the way our brains work, losing some of what we encode is inevitable. You won't correctly encode everything you look at. If you try to encode everything, it will take you forever to read through the material. More likely, you'll fail to encode some stuff or you'll encode something wrong. The consequences of forgetting a piece of information are usually no worse than failing to encode it in the first place. Reading every single word in a book, article, or anything else is much more time-consuming and more difficult, at least for me, than filtering that information. And yet, it comes with the same risk of forgetting. So you may as well filter. It's easier to do, and it's easier on your brain—and you may need that extra brainpower later.

In fact, maybe you're already filtering *this* book. Or you're tempted to start filtering, now that I've planted the seed. No worries; I've already filtered for you. That's why each chapter concludes with "Encode This," a quick recap of its most important points. Of course, what you and I deem important may be entirely different. So you might want to keep reading the whole book, just in case.

There's one other potential problem with filtering—and it's a big one. In times of great stress, filtering becomes *way* more difficult. When the stakes are high, it's scary to think you might inadvertently filter out a critical piece of information. And because you're upset and distracted, that risk only increases.

Over the course of Jeanne's illness, she endured various treatments and surgeries. She went to see different doctors, she stayed in various hospitals. Each week, it seemed as if countless new symptoms—and strategies for dealing with them—appeared. Almost from the beginning, it was hard to understand all the medical information we were receiving; it was beyond the frame of reference we had. Doctors would tell us things, but given the enormous strain we were under, neither Jeanne nor I would remember them clearly.

Her illness was challenging enough without the added stress of having to deal with this avalanche of information. Even with great doctors and patient advocates, I was constantly confused and frightened—and I wasn't even the one who was sick. The hopelessness we felt at being so overwhelmed by all the information we were receiving made everything seem worse.

The point is, whatever ordeal you may face, filtering information will be a challenge. But it's still important—probably more so than ever. This is why I recommend that you begin practicing filtering, in whatever way makes sense to you, now, before you're faced with a crisis. It's inevitable that at some point in your life, there will come a time when you suddenly have to make sense of extremely important information that's foreign to you, and you may not have your full mental faculties available to help you do it. If you've got a filtering practice already in place, you have a better chance at making some sense of it all and then, of being "the cooler head that prevails."

ENCODE THIS

- Given the massive amount of information coming at you every day, it's important to keep in your head only what truly needs to be there. The first step toward getting rid of that clutter is *filtering*.

- To filter, try to decide what your goals are for the information before or as you read it. Skim through the material, whether it's a book, article, blog post, or a string of e-mails. Use your goals to group the information into categories depending on what you need to do with the information: ignore it, store it to come back to later, or encode it into memory. You might also consider grouping the information you want to store or encode into smaller categories based on its context.

- Knowing your goals for information helps you organize it. It also helps you remember it because if you know how you plan to use a piece of information later, you can develop a context or story for the information, which helps with encoding.

- Filtering is more difficult when you don't have goals. But it can be done. Repetition and rereading will usually help you identify goals for the information.

- Repetition, either through writing something down or rereading it, also enhances recall. Dedicate time each week to reviewing information you've collected during that week—meeting notes, e-mail, Web pages you bookmarked, and so on. Reviewing the information again, at a time when you're focused, will help you remember it. When you can easily recall information you need, when you need it, you'll be more organized and successful.

- Break big chunks of information (or actions) into smaller ones, whenever possible. You won't feel so overwhelmed. And it will increase your chances of remembering. Plus, it will allow you to look for patterns and themes so you can organize the chunks in a way that, given your goals, makes the most sense to you.

- Start practicing your own version of filtering as soon as possible. It'll help you be more prepared later, should you have to deal with an onslaught of information during a crisis.

chapter 8

DAY-TIMER OR DIGITAL?

when, and when not, to go paperless

EXCUSE ME IF I'M asking a personal question. But what's your relationship with paper like these days?

Mine's a bit complicated. And it might even surprise you. For example, I still prefer to receive financial statements on paper and in the mail, even though pretty much everything is available for e-delivery. At the same time, I take meeting notes in Google Docs (an online word processing program), when others may still use spiral-bound notebooks.

All of us have information we need to keep but don't need to store in our heads. And we use a combination of paper and digital tools for the job. But with all the various options and tools available to us today for storing information, and with all the information we consume and create, how do we choose which tool for which job? It's not always easy to know, but this chapter can help.

First of all, it's important to recognize that a number of factors influence how we choose to receive, store, and organize information. But those factors don't always steer us to the best or most efficient tool.

Generational preferences can come into play. A fifty-year-old may still read print newspapers, even though she's tech savvy and the entire paper is available online for free. But she grew up reading a print newspaper, every day, so that's how she prefers to get her news—even if the newspapers clutter up her living room and kill trees.

Engrained habits are another factor. As I noted in chapter 2, often we cling to systems simply because they're familiar, even if they aren't optimal. We fear change, or we're convinced that doing something differently will require more energy or time than it's worth. For the longest time, Sonya was devoted to her Day-Timer paper calendar/organizer, and she didn't see any reason to give it up for a digital calendar system. She didn't see the benefit in spending the time to learn a digital system, even if it could have better met her needs.

Then there are our emotional attachments. We form (sometimes unhealthy) relationships with our Day-Timers, Black-Berrys, iPhones, and laptops. These attachments may prevent us from making the best decision when it comes to how we organize our information. Despite what you may think, digital devices aren't, in fact, always the best tools for storing and organizing information (in this chapter I'll help you figure out when they are and aren't the best tools for the situation).

Finally, lack of trust is another influence. Interestingly, we tend to distrust paper and digital tools alike. Often, we worry that if we put important information in the cloud or on a computer, some nasty virus or server crash will wipe it out forever. Or we fret that if we write something by hand, we'll lose the piece of paper it's written on. Whatever the anxiety is, it can cause us to use the wrong tool for the job.

As I say, our relationship with paper can get complicated. But, fearless readers, it's important we figure out this paper versus digital question because when we don't have a clear strategy for dealing with information we need to keep, we do things the wrong way. We may lose information or end up doing the same thing more than once. We might show up for an appointment on the wrong day or forget someone's birthday—all of which can cause stress. Plus, when we're disorganized, we may not be able to share important information with others. Everybody loses in that scenario.

Pardon me while I burst into flames.

—Incubus, "Pardon Me"

So how do you develop your organizational systems so that you're using the right tool for each task? I'd start by objectively assessing the tools and methods you're already using. Make a list of all the different tools you use and how you use them. Keep in mind that anything you rely on to help organize your life is a tool: sticky notes, iPhone applications, inboxes (physical or digital), that string around your finger—anything. Then challenge your assumptions about why you do things the way you do. Try to identify where and how your systems let you down—after all, every organizational system has its breaking point. In fact, my organizational principle no. 16 says: *There's no such thing as a perfect system of organization.* The goal isn't to devise a perfect system, because you can't. A better plan is to try to identify the breaking points and figure out a way to work around them.

> **There's no such thing as a perfect system of organization.**

Once again, your goals will guide you. The goals you have for a piece of information can help you decide how to store or organize that information. When I'm trying to decide which tool to use, I'll ask myself a few questions about my goals for that information, such as: Why do I need the information?

How, when, and where might I use it later? How long will I need it? Who, aside from me, could benefit from it?

For example, I travel frequently for business. When I do, there's a lot of information I need to have with me—the number of my flight, departure and arrival times, my seat assignment, the name and address of the hotel where I'll be staying, and so on. I could try, and probably fail, to memorize all that, but that's more trouble than it's worth. I could keep it all stored on my iPhone or laptop, but there are times during travel when I can't turn them on. Instead, I forward any e-mails relating to my trip, such as airline itineraries, to Sonya, so she'll have a copy. I print a copy of my itinerary to keep in my carry-on bag for easy reference. I take a printout of my hotel confirmation too, in case I need to show it to the front desk clerk. If all else fails, I still have access to those e-mails from my iPhone. And because I never delete e-mails (unless they're obviously spam), I can search my previous travel itineraries again later, if I need to look something up.

This is just one small example of how various paper and digital tools can each serve an important, though different, purpose. The trick is in knowing which are best for which job. In this chapter, I'll show you how and when I use paper, and where it lets me down. Then, in chapters 9, 10, and 11, I'll explain which digital tools I use to store and organize which types of information, and why.

The Uses of Paper

Getting stuff out of your head. One reason I like paper is because it helps me get stuff out of my head. If I have a million thoughts buzzing around, I feel so much better when I scribble them down on paper. Once they're recorded, I stop worrying about them. Even if I don't actually do anything about them, my stress level drops, and I'm able to focus.

I know: I can do all this on a computer. Sometimes I do. But somehow, it's not the same. Paper just feels more tangible, definitive, and cathartic. I like to use paper to jot down ideas that come to me randomly, or questions that are nagging me, usually when I'm on the go. Another benefit of using paper is that I can write something down in a small notepad just about anytime or anywhere. That's not true with my laptop, which I don't always have with me, or my iPhone, which is great for reading information but not so hot (because of the on-screen keyboard) for actually typing it.

Solving problems. There's something about paper that helps me brainstorm too. When I'm trying to solve a complex problem or understand something challenging, I write things out on huge Post-it Easel Pad sheets. I've been known to place the big sticky sheets all over my living room wall. Then I move them around into different arrangements. I even tear off pieces and tape them into different sections. When I'm lucky, a Eureka! moment ensues.

There are reasons why this technique works. Moving the pieces around physically allows my brain to make connections and see solutions it might otherwise have missed. Sure, I could do all this on a computer, and I have—as I explained in the last chapter. But as of this moment in time, I don't own a computer screen as large as a wall. Having all that space to move my thoughts around on paper is freeing and allows me to see much more information in one glance.

You might try this yourself. You could simply rip sheets off a notepad and tape them to your wall. Or buy one of those giant dry-erase boards for your office. Giving yourself that physical space to shuffle around information and try out ideas can stimulate your thinking in ways that staring at a computer monitor might not. That's why I recommend using paper to capture ideas and information you need for solving problems, as opposed to information you just need to passively refer to.

Digesting a lot of written information. I also prefer paper when I have to read and react to something. For example, when writing this book, I printed every chapter multiple times. I marked up drafts of each chapter as I read them and wrote notes in the margins. Then I typed my notes into the chapter's text file and e-mailed it to Jim. Is this the fastest way of writing a book? I doubt it. It's certainly not the greenest solution either. (Don't worry; I'm a devout recycler.) But working on paper helps me see things I might have missed on a computer screen. I can rip the papers apart and put paragraphs or pages into different orders without having to recall which pieces have been copied and pasted in my text file.

Receiving financial statements. Financial statements are another category of information I still prefer to store and organize on paper (at least for now).

"Really?" you're probably thinking. "The former Google CIO gets his financial statements *in the mail*?" Yes. And you too might want to reconsider all those e-statements you signed up for.

Let's step back for a second and think about it in terms of goals. Why do you get financial statements at all? The goals I have for my financial statements are as follows:

1. To make sure nothing's amiss in my accounts.

2. To hand the statements over later to my tax preparer (who requires paper documents for his records).

3. To archive them after taxes for up to seven years to meet Internal Revenue Service requirements. (The IRS mandates that taxpayers keep financial records from three to seven years or even indefinitely, depending on "the action, expense or event the document records."[1])

Receiving my financial statements on paper serves my first two goals extremely well. A paper document that comes in the mail is by default easy to review: I just open the envelope it came in. Plus, it arrives at regular intervals, which serves as a visual reminder that it's time to view my statement (or pay a bill). Could I sign up for e-notifications alerting me when my statement is ready for viewing? Sure. But let me ask you this: How many e-mails do you get per day (compared with pieces of physical mail)? How often do you actually read all the automatically generated ones, from places like your bank? Also, my accountant wants all my financial records on paper. Because my statements come in the mail, all I've got to do is file them so I can find them easily later when it's time to mail them to my accountant.

For the sake of argument, let's say I opted for e-statements instead of receiving statements in the mail. To get each month's statement, I'd have to look up my user ID and password for the financial institution's Web site; log into my account; dig my way toward the links to my current e-statement; and download the statement to my computer. When it's tax time, I'd need to print and mail the statements to my tax preparer or, at a minimum, e-mail them to him and make him print them. And multiply this by however many accounts I hold (if you're like me, you probably have more than one). Point is, by going through all those steps, I've created extra work for myself—*which is the exact opposite of being efficient.*

My system of receiving statements on paper has its disadvantages, of course. For starters, there's a chance I may misfile a document, whereas a digital copy would be easy to search for on my computer. In fact, not long ago, I couldn't find a particular financial statement I'd received in the mail. I had to call the financial institution and request a duplicate. It took so long to arrive, I had to file for an extension on my tax return.

And of course, as you know, filing cabinets have an annoying tendency to overflow. So how do you physically—and securely—store seven years' worth of paper documents?

I have a system to work around that particular breaking point. When my file cabinet starts to fill up, I simply sift through the contents. Financial or other sensitive information I no longer need, I shred. Other stuff goes into recycling. I store files I don't refer to frequently but might need later in a filing box, label the box on all sides, and store the box in my basement or other out-of-the-way, secure place. Admittedly, this is time-consuming but worth it.

If this system of keeping paper documents and periodically weeding out your filing cabinet doesn't work for you, though, there are other ways you can minimize paper's limitations. You could scan each paper financial statement into a PDF file after you first review it, then store it electronically.

(PDF files retain the look and feel of the original document. And they're searchable, as long as you've put them through the optical character recognition process.)

Or you could e-mail the PDF to yourself, so you'd have the digital copy archived in your e-mail account. As further backup, you could also file the paper statement in its appropriate folder in your filing cabinet drawer dedicated to financial stuff, to keep for your tax preparer. Then, after seven years, you could feed those paper statements into a shredder.

Anyhow, I'll keep receiving my financial statements in the mail for now, thank you very much. And it's not just because this is how I've always done things. It's because I'm letting my goals determine how I receive and store this information, instead of simply accepting someone else's system that doesn't meet my needs.

Storing legal documents. Legal documents are another form of information I still receive on paper, as I recommend you do too. For one thing, it's much easier to verify the authenticity of a signature or seal on paper. And many government and other agencies still accept only paper documents. I'd recommend keeping your most important legal papers (such as wills, power of attorney documents, and contracts) in a safe or bank safety deposit box. Try to get PDFs of these documents too. (Usually, law firms will supply PDFs of signed contracts, though you may have to pay extra.) The PDFs aren't of great value as legal documents per se, but they do serve as a quick, searchable reference. If you can't easily get a PDF of an important legal document, scan it. If you don't have a scanner, you can use one at a copy center or office supply store.

Because legal documents are so important, and they can be difficult (and costly) to replace, I send an e-mail to my Gmail address, reminding me where I've stored an important legal document on paper. I attach the PDF of the document to the e-mail reminder of where I stored the original. On the e-mail, I also copy anyone else who might need access to the document, like Sonya.

Many organization experts will tell you that, like an empty e-mail inbox, a clean desk is the holy grail of organization. They'll tell you an empty work surface gives you the freedom to start fresh every day, to think more clearly, to be more productive.

I'm here to tell you a different story.

My home office desk is covered with stacks of paper, which are, in turn, often tagged with sticky notes. If that isn't enough, my office walls are usually covered with large sheets of paper. If you walked into my office, in fact, you might find that the office belonging to the author of a book on organization looks, well, kinda disorganized. But it's not—at least, it's not disorganized for me.

It's just a fact that paper—whether it's notes, bills, lists, or faxes—comes into my life, whether I want it or not. So if my goal were to keep my desk completely free of papers, I'd have to be able to predict when, and for what purpose, I'd later need those papers at the time I received them. This would require me to be the Amazing Kreskin, something at which I'm doomed to fail.

If I were able to achieve Kreskin status, I'd still have to stop everything I was doing at the time, even if I were busy focusing on other things, which I usually am, and either file or discard each of those pieces of paper, right then and there. This would force me to shift contexts, which is not only distracting but also brain taxing over time (more about context shifting in chapter 12). To me, that's a whole lot of work, just to get to a clean work surface.

Instead, I accept the fact that I often don't have time to deal with papers when I receive them; it's a constraint I work around. So I arrange the papers on my desk in stacks according to contexts or goals. For example, one stack might be a variety of offers received in the mail I want to save, like a coupon to a sporting goods store or a film festival

(cont.)

Day-Timer or Digital?

catalog. Another might be financial documents that need to be reviewed and then recycled or shredded. A third might be magazines I read on the plane, with articles I want to keep or reread tagged with colored sticky notes. And all reminders, notes, or bits of information I don't want to bury in a stack (like frequently used passwords or phone numbers) get written on sticky notes, which I put in plain view so I can refer to them whenever I need to.

My system frees me from having to take action on a paper when it's inconvenient or my mind is in the wrong context (I still have to put papers in the relevant stacks, of course, but that takes very minimal thought and effort). Also, these stacks of paper serve as their own visual reminders that, oh yeah, I've got stuff I need to do. If those papers weren't sitting on my desk (or sticking to my wall), I guarantee you, I'd forget about them. In most cases, once I've taken the necessary action, the paper is no longer important to me, and into the shredder it goes. Maybe that's why my home office has only one filing cabinet drawer full of files (which are mostly recent financial and legal stuff I have to keep).

So rather than striving for a work surface devoid of papers, my advice is to simply group those papers by their contexts, the goals you have for them, or the actions they require of you in a way that ensures you won't forget them. It doesn't matter if it *looks* a little messy, as long as you're using your physical workspace in a way that makes sense to you. *That*'s what I call being organized.

The Downsides to Paper

To summarize: Paper is great for taking quick notes on the go; for brainstorming and problem solving; and for storing financial and legal documents. In other situations, however, paper often goes to the back of the class. Here are the times I *don't* recommend using paper.

When you have a lot of it. Whenever you have a lot of information arranged in no particular order, paper is not your friend. You can't quickly search for information when it's stored on paper the way you can when that information is stored in digital format. When it's on paper, you can only hunt for it in a place where you think it's likely to be, which, as we've discussed, we're terrible at doing. Plus, paper notebooks, documents, and file folders take up physical space. It's cheaper and more practical to store as much information as you can on a hard drive or in the cloud than it is to dedicate space to filing cabinets in a high-rent office.

When you don't know where or when you'll need it. Storing your information in digital format also gives you more flexibility than storing it on paper. With digital tools, you don't have to predict when, how, or where you'll want that information in the future.

For example, imagine it's late at night. You're reviewing a presentation you'll be giving early the next morning. Suddenly, you get an idea for several points you'd like to make. Unfortunately, the information that supports those points is on a paper document in your office, which is a thirty-minute drive away. Now you're facing a truly heinous choice: Drive to the office and back tonight, which will waste an hour of your time? Or get to work even earlier the next morning to update your presentation? Both options pretty much ensure you'll lose sleep, though you'd probably lose more in the second scenario. Either way, this isn't the kind of choice I like.

If you'd stored that information digitally, however, and brought your company laptop home that night, you'd most likely have the information you suddenly decided you needed. Cool; just add it to your presentation and it's off to bed you go. Even if you forgot to bring the laptop, you may still be okay. As long as your documents are stored in the cloud (with an online backup service or a Web-based service like Google Docs), or they're available through remote access, you can use your home computer to grab them. (With a remote access service, you can retrieve files stored on one computer using a different computer.)

I'd also advocate using digital tools to securely store or back up any information that's confidential or in any way irreplaceable. I remember some particularly powerful footage from the day after Hurricane Ike hit Texas in September 2008. A CNN reporter was on camera roaming downtown Houston. You could see skyscrapers with blown-out windows in the background, and sheets of paper blowing around on the street. The reporter picked up one of the paper documents littering the streets and showed it to the camera. It was marked "Confidential."

This is not the fate you want for your confidential documents. Granted, hurricanes and other disasters are relatively rare, and many of those documents littering downtown Houston were probably printouts of computer files. But there's another concern that this news report raised: After a disaster or unforeseen event, you might not be able to return to the office anytime soon to get information stored on paper (like customer records). If your information is stored in the cloud or backed up offsite, however, you can rebound from a serious business disruption more quickly.

The answer my friend / Is blowin' in the wind.
—Bob Dylan, "Blowin' in the Wind"

When others might need it. Information you need to share with other people is often best stored in digital form too, instead of on paper. Digital information is just easier to share than paper. For example, you can simply e-mail a digital document to someone, or you can give that person access to a shared folder on your computer. Also, most people can open and read digital files in standard formats, like Word or PDF documents. But handwritten information on paper can be illegible to others (even *I* can't read my handwriting sometimes).

When you care about the environment. Last but not least, the problem with paper is that it comes from trees. Storing information digitally, on the other hand, requires using computers and servers, which use energy but still have a comparatively smaller carbon footprint.

Benefits of the Cloud

Digital files have their own drawbacks too, of course. For one thing, digital formats are always changing, and files stored on outdated media, such as the nearly extinct floppy disk, can be difficult to access. Or maybe you backed up some files on DVDs instead of floppies. But does anyone really know how long a DVD lasts? And how long until that storage system is rendered obsolete by a better one, like flash drive storage?

There is a solution to this problem: It's called the cloud. If you store your most important information online, as long as you have a computer and an Internet connection, you can get to your files, without worrying about hardware obsolescence. One caveat: Use a reputable online storage or backup service. Why? Because in difficult economic times, some of the more obscure services may be discontinued. In early 2009, for instance, users of some soon-to-be-defunct online storage services were sent scrambling to download their files before a deadline, after which their files would be erased. So choose a service from a company unlikely to disappear—those should be around for a while. For example, Microsoft offers a service called Windows Live SkyDrive (skydrive.live.com), which currently lets you store up to 25GB of data. I use Dropbox (getdropbox.com) to provide an online backup of various files that matter to me. As I'll describe later, I also use Gmail itself as a way of providing backups. (More on DropBox can be found in the "Stuff We Love" appendix.)

There's just no way of knowing, ultimately, how long your information will be accessible in a digital format. You can hedge your bets a bit by keeping multiple copies of the most important stuff on DVDs, hard drives, and in the cloud. Make sure you give your spouse, kids, or close friends access to your important digital files, in case of emergency.

The Importance of Taking Notes

As you can see, the question of when to use paper isn't cut and dry. Let's look at note taking, for example. As I mentioned, in terms of convenience, paper still can't be beat for making quick notes when you're away from your computer, which is why I carry around a little Moleskine notebook. Naturally, I sometimes can't remember in which notebook I wrote something. And I can't do a quick search to find it. But there you have it in a nutshell: the pros and cons of paper.

You can minimize the downsides of keeping notes in various notebooks by dedicating each one to a specific subject matter. For example, you could keep one notebook specifically for health matters. It's important to take notes during a doctor's visit, while the information is still in your short-term memory. But typing on a computer or on a BlackBerry during a checkup, especially if you're only wearing socks, is deeply awkward. A paper notebook fills the need nicely.

Before each trip to see the doctor, you might spend a few minutes reviewing notes from your previous visits. Write down questions you want to ask in your upcoming appointment, and then jot down the answers your doctor gives you during your visit. In between visits, make a note whenever you have a cold, a flu, allergic reaction, or whatever, so you'll have that information handy during a checkup. You could use colored sticky notes as tabbed dividers too, so you could quickly organize your notes by date, symptom, or anything else that's important to track. Visits to the doctor can be extremely stressful (as I was reminded during Jeanne's illness), so it's critical to take the best notes possible and organize them so you can find them easily later.

I keep a notepad or a Moleskine notebook near my computer too, specifically for jotting quick notes. Usually, the notes are related to voicemail messages. It's an easy way to jot down phone numbers and to-do items. Yes, I know: I could type these on my computer so I could search for that information later. But scribbling on paper as I listen to voicemail is easier, to my mind.

However, neither method is ideal for taking notes from voicemail. A better method is to use a voicemail-to-text transcription service, which automatically transcribes voicemails into text for you. The text is then sent to you as an e-mail, with an audio file of the original voicemail attached. Some services use actual humans to do the transcribing; some rely entirely on technology; and others use a combination of both. Either way, the transcriptions are generally accurate enough to tell you at least the gist of a caller's message.

Voicemail-to-text services have lots of advantages. For one, reading—or, more accurately, skimming—them is much faster than listening to the typical (oh, let's be honest: rambling) voicemail. For another, getting all your messages by checking e-mail, instead of having to check both voicemail *and* e-mail, saves time. And, when transcribed into text, the voicemail becomes part of your searchable e-mail archive forever—instead of being lost to the ages because your phone company forced you to delete it after a month or two. It's also much easier to forward an e-mail than it is a voicemail. Because the voicemail is now text, you can delete irrelevant parts or add your own comments before forwarding the message. Plus, if a caller left a phone number in the voicemail, you can cut and paste it into your contacts, instead of having to listen to it three times to make out all the digits. (Have you noticed how people will talk slowly and clearly for the entire voicemail message, *until* it's time for them to leave their number—then they sprint through the number like it's an Olympic event?) Usually, you can even click the number in the transcribed voicemail and your cell phone will automatically dial it.

A voicemail-to-e-mail transcription service can save you time and effort in lots of other ways too, especially if you're creative. For example, instead of tapping out a memo to yourself on your cell phone or computer, you could simply call and leave yourself a voicemail. The service will transcribe your message into text and send it to you, where it becomes part of your searchable e-mail archive.

When Jim and I began writing this book, he set up a dedicated phone number with a voicemail-to-e-mail transcription service. The idea was to give me a way to capture random thoughts related to the book as they occurred to me. Rather than carrying around a digital voice recorder, then having to get my recording to Jim, I just used the cell phone I've always got with me. When I had an idea, I'd dial the dedicated phone number and start talking after the beep. Within a few minutes, Jim would receive my message transcribed into e-mail, with the original recording attached as an audio file. It saved him from having to transcribe my messages, it gave him a searchable archive of my messages, and it saved me time and effort.

Naturally, there are some downsides to voicemail-to-e-mail services. Some cost money, though not a lot. And the transcription accuracy can vary. If you are calling from a noisy place, like an airport departure lounge, the transcription isn't going to be as accurate as it would be if you were calling from a quiet office. Still, it's the fastest and easiest way to capture notes from voicemail, as well as to record notes for yourself and others.

I'll never be the same.

—Incubus, "Pardon Me"

Whatever Happened to the Paperless Office?

Time-out for a trivia question. The sentence "Some believe that the paperless office is not that far off" appeared in a *BusinessWeek* article published in which year?

a. 1975

b. 1997

c. 2001

The correct answer is (may we have a drum roll, please?)... 1975.[2] Yes, folks, we've been bouncing the "paperless office" concept around for over three decades. So with all the advances in digital technology since the heyday of disco, why haven't we gone paperless by now?

Get down tonight.

—K.C. & The Sunshine Band, "Get Down Tonight"

I think it has to do with what I explained in chapter 2: We're so resistant to changing our systems that we cling to them even when the goals behind the systems have shifted and/or the systems aren't working anymore because technology or societal shifts have made them obsolete. For decades, paper has been at the heart of our workflows. So even though paper is no longer always the most effective (or environmentally sound) way to store information, we're reluctant to abandon it, even when we should.

Case in point: Sonya. For over ten years, she used a Day-Timer faithfully (for those of you who don't know, a Day-Timer is a personal organizer, sort of like a bound-book version of a PDA). When she worked for a public relations agency in the nineties, she tracked billable time spent on each client on her Day-Timer's calendar. Sonya grew accustomed to using her organizer for storing to-do list items, addresses, and scribbled notes. It was a comfortable, familiar system she trusted.

Sonya liked having her to-do list on the left side of her Day-Timer and her calendar on the right. "I have a really visual memory," she explained. "Having my to-dos and calendar arranged like that helped me picture everything in my head, and that helped me remember."

Then, disaster struck. Sonya lost her Day-Timer. She called every place she'd been before losing it. She struggled to re-create the information she'd lost. She was in agony for weeks and was even reduced to tears.

> **Don't try to deny what you feel.**
> —Disturbed, "Down with the Sickness"

Sonya replaced her Day-Timer with another one, though she briefly flirted with and rejected a Palm PDA. "Technology just doesn't interest me," Sonya said. She didn't see the benefit of spending the time and energy to learn a digital tool when a paper organization system, despite its obvious drawbacks, suited her just fine.

Everyone kept trying to talk her out of her Day-Timer, but she was stubborn—she used to say I'd have to pry her Day-Timer out of her cold, dead hands. Fortunately, that wasn't necessary. I gave her an iPhone and a MacBook instead.

We entered her contacts into Apple's MobileMe address book (apple.com/mobileme); MobileMe services include an address book, calendar, and e-mail. Now, Sonya can access all her phone numbers, addresses, and notes about the people in her address book from her phone, and any computer with a Web browser. She doesn't have to worry about losing that information again. In what I consider to be an amazing triumph of technology, 2009 was the first year since the mid-1990s that Sonya didn't buy a Day-Timer refill pack.

Let's take another example of a system in which many people continue to use paper even though it's no longer optimal: corporate travel.

At least one aspect of the entire business travel process has gone paperless. Instead of paper tickets, we now get e-tickets, which are way more convenient. All you need to do is show up at the airport with your ID and the credit card to which you charged the ticket. (I also recommend taking a suitcase.) The airlines save money on paper and postage. You don't have to wait for a ticket to arrive by mail or worry about losing it. Everyone wins.

Even so, some companies still require that travel requests and approvals be submitted on paper. Originally, their goal was to ensure that employees didn't jet off to New York for "training" (wink, wink) or Kauai for a "sales conference" (nudge, nudge). That's a good goal. But I'd argue that it wouldn't be too difficult to come up with a paperless system for travel approval.

In its earlier days, Google used to require employees to submit a trail of paper forms to be reimbursed for expenses. Eventually, the company simplified the system. If you needed to travel for business, you'd send your manager an e-mail, explaining when you were traveling and why. When you returned from your trip, you'd print the e-mail thread and submit it with receipts in order to get reimbursed. Ultimately, we simplified it even further: You just scanned your receipts in and mailed the resulting PDF along with your expense report. It was a beautifully simple, effective system. But time marches on. By the time I left Google, it was a much bigger company, with a more complex employee travel reimbursement process involving lots of database entries and multiple approvals. And sadly it involved more paper.

Ultimately, the reason many businesses don't adopt paperless systems for things like travel approvals isn't because they don't trust it or don't see the benefit; it's because they resist change. The result: The travel approval process consumes more employee effort and time than necessary. We're not talking about a lot, mind you. Still, it's time and effort that could have been spent on more profitable activities. When you pile another inefficient system on top of all the other ones, the costs begin to add up.

An Awkward Transition

As of this moment in time, we're probably somewhere in the middle of the paper-to-digital transition. And it's confusing because we can't figure out which way to turn. But guess what? The powers that be—banks and financial institutions, schools, employers, government agencies—haven't made the transition any easier for us. That's because, all too often, they're still applying the old ways of paper to digital documents.

Same as it ever was.

—Talking Heads, "Once in a Lifetime"

Awkward transitions like this are the norm, sad to say. Think about the big transitions in the media. The first radio programs were often nothing more than people delivering news and ads—the same things daily newspapers had been doing for years. Similarly, the earliest TV shows, especially low-budget local programs, often showed announcers planted in front of microphones, reading news and mentioning sponsors, just as they'd done on radio. More recently, many podcasts were (some still are) merely people reading their blogs or something else they'd written.

Running in circles / Chasing our tails.

—Coldplay, "The Scientist"

This is all understandable. These were huge transitions, and it can take a while to absorb big changes. But when we don't adapt our old ways of communicating to better suit a new medium, we fail to exploit all the possibilities and benefits inherent to that medium.

The transition we're in, from paper to digital documents, is no different. Let's return to financial statements for an example, because the transition from paper to digital in this regard has been particularly painful.

My checking account is actually a money market fund. As such, my paper statements list countless securities traded in my account the previous month. Honestly, I don't care about those transactions. I just want to verify that the checks I wrote have cleared and the deposits I made have been recorded.

I could go to my financial institution's Web site, select the start and finish dates for the period I'm interested in, and view my deposits and debits online. But I can't download the information this way. Instead, I must download a digital version of my entire paper statement, including all those transactions I don't care about. It's hugely frustrating because the leaders at this particular financial institution haven't thought about how to take advantage of digital information delivery. The capability exists to offer different options for downloading, allowing customers to pick and choose which information they'd like on their e-statement. But they haven't considered how their customers would actually like to receive this information and how they could satisfy those needs using the new medium of digital statements. Instead, the institution simply provides the same old statement it does on paper, only in digital format.

Paper's Still Important, But...

As you see, despite my fondness for technology, and my belief that digital devices are often the most efficient way to store information, paper remains an important part of my life. Old-fashioned as it might sound, paper is at the core of some tried-and-true organizational systems I've developed, like filtering information with colored pens and highlighters. Those systems got me through difficult times, helped me overcome the challenges of dyslexia, and enabled me to succeed in academia, and later on, in the business world.

That said, I realize that paper systems come with some built-in failure. I also know that in a lot of areas, we as a society need to move beyond paper because some of the ways we use it cause us to spend time and energy that could be used elsewhere.

Did I mention my relationship with paper is complicated? I'm not here to tell you when you should and shouldn't use paper over a digital device. That's a decision only you can make. My larger point here is that when you do make these decisions, keep in mind your goals and objectives for the information. Determine when you'll most likely need the information, how you'll use it, how long you'll need to keep it, and whom you might want to share it with. Then come up with a logical, convenient system you can stick to.

Just remember, it's rarely a good idea to keep doing something a certain way simply because it's how you've always done it. In fact, as we learned in chapter 2, that's typically a *bad* idea. Instead, resolve to use paper or digital tools based on *authentic* goals for the information you receive or record, not on emotional attachments, engrained habits, generational preferences, or fears. If you truly want to be more efficient, challenge the ways you've been organizing the information in your world and open yourself to new ways of doing it.

ENCODE THIS

It's difficult to decide when to use paper or digital tools to organize personal information, for several reasons:

- Paper is a great tool for getting stuff into and out of our heads. But it has plenty of limitations too, especially when compared to digital information storage.

- Emotions, engrained habits, generational preferences, and trust issues also influence which tools we choose for organizing information.

- We're in the middle of a transition between paper and digital tools. And the powers that be aren't making it easier for us. Too often, digital documents are simply electronic versions of paper documents, and they fail to exploit the ways in which the new medium could better meet our needs.

- Whenever possible, use your goals for the information in your life to guide how you should store that information—whether on paper or in a digital format.

WHEN TO USE PAPER

- Paper is a great way to brainstorm. When your goal is to solve a problem or come up with ideas, write your thoughts down on Post-it Easel Pads, cut and paste pieces, and move them closer together to help you see patterns and themes develop. Dry-erase boards work well too.

- When your goal is to encode or really absorb information, print documents instead of reading them on screen. You may notice things on paper you wouldn't have caught on a computer monitor.

- When you have a lot of things buzzing around in your head, write them down on paper. It's cathartic and helps you clear your mind.

- Make sure that having information in digital format is truly more efficient than paper. Financial statements are a classic example. It takes more work to manage financial statements in digital format than it does in their paper versions.

- Keep legal documents on paper in a safe place. But also send yourself an e-mail reminder of where you've stored the documents. Attach a PDF version of the document to the e-mail too. Send the e-mail to anyone who should have a copy of the document and should know where the original is filed.

- Carry around a small notebook. You may need it to make a quick note when you aren't able to do so on a computer or over the phone.

WHEN TO CHOOSE A DIGITAL TOOL OVER PAPER

- When you have a lot of random information or you need to share the information with others, storing information digitally is preferable to keeping it on paper. You can access it in more ways, you're less likely to misplace it, and you'll be able to share and search the information easily.

- Although you should keep paper versions of important or confidential documents (such as wills and contracts), always back them up digitally, in case the original gets lost or destroyed. The digital version also acts as a quick, searchable reference.

- Consider moving your most important documents to the cloud, so you won't have to worry later about having stored them on an obsolete storage media.

- If possible, use a voicemail-to-e-mail transcription service. It will keep you from having to jot down notes while listening to voice messages. And it provides a written, searchable archive of your messages that's easy to share with others.

chapter 9

BEYOND SEND & RECEIVE

turning your e-mails into a searchable
history that's all about you

SINCE INFORMATION IS VITAL to being organized, it stands to reason that the easier it is to get to your information, the better your chances are of being organized. That's why I believe it's important to store as much of your information as possible in the cloud. But doing so requires you to think a bit differently about the information in your life—how you store it, how and when you access it. That's okay; in fact, that's one of the objectives of this book—to encourage you to think differently about the digital information you're accumulating.

In my case, rather than regard it as a bunch of disparate, disconnected piles of data, I think of my digital information as a single entity—specifically, as a building that's always expanding. And I call the tools I use to add to or access that information *scaffolds.*

As you know, a scaffold is a platform that surrounds a multifloor building under construction (or renovation). It gives workers quick and easy access to the building's exterior, as well as to any floor inside the building. Similarly, the majority of scaffolds I use in the digital world—such as Gmail, Google's e-mail service—give me quick, easy access to my ever-growing information.

A scaffold isn't a particular piece of equipment, like a laptop or iPhone, though those tools allow me to use my scaffolds. And a scaffold does much more than a search engine, though search is part of what makes most of many scaffolds so useful. A scaffold is any tool that lets me store, search, organize, and access the digital information I want or need to keep but don't really need to encode. And the best part is that I can personalize my scaffolds to match the way I think, work, and live.

When reading the new few chapters, you'll notice that many of my scaffolds, such as Gmail and Google Calendar, are by Google. At Google, we were expected to "eat our own dog food," to use only Google products for e-mail, calendar, and such. Even though I left Google in early 2008, I believe Google tools continue to be the best for what they do, and they're constantly being improved and enhanced. I don't use Google products because I used to work there, though I certainly learned the ins and outs of them during my time at Google. Rather, I use Google tools because they fit nicely with my core beliefs about how we need to organize our information today—that is, the needs to store our information in a central place, to share it easily with others, and to use powerful search to find what we need, when we need it. These are the reasons why I continue to rely on Google tools as much as possible. (And for what it's worth, neither Sonya nor I are Google shareholders.) However, in the "Stuff We

Love" appendix at the end of this book, you'll find alternatives to my scaffolds.

So that's what the next three chapters are about: the scaffolds I use to access and organize my digital information, why I use them, and how they help me become better organized. This chapter is about Gmail. In chapter 10, I'll talk about Google Calendar and a to-do list program called Things. Chapter 11 is about the scaffolds I use for managing documents and information I find online. Please keep in mind as you read the next few chapters that the technology I describe here may have changed since I wrote the text.

Gmail: It's All About You

There's never been anything else quite like e-mail. The work projects you've completed, the plans you've made, the conversations you've had, the corny jokes you've laughed at but shouldn't have—they're all part of this amazing, searchable historical archive that's all about you. In a sense, your e-mail archive is your biography in collage form, composed of countless fragments from multiple contributors (including you).

As indispensable as e-mail has become, you need the right tools to really tap its full potential. There are loads of e-mail systems for reaching out and touching someone electronically, of course: Gmail, Microsoft Outlook (which works independently or as the e-mail/calendaring program that connects to the Microsoft Exchange Server in the corporate environment), Lotus Notes, Thunderbird, MSN Hotmail, and Yahoo! Mail, to name a few.

The best e-mail system is the one that lets me quickly sort and search through years of messages. It's accessible from any computer or any Internet-connected phone. It's the one that's easiest to use and has a huge amount of free storage, so I never have to delete old messages to make room for new ones. It excels at filtering out spam.

That's Gmail.

Gmail (mail.google.com) is the scaffold I use most often. (Anyone with a free Google account can use Gmail and any other Google product.) On one level, I use Gmail the way everyone else does: to send and receive e-mail. But what a lot of people don't realize is that Gmail can do so much more. For example, I also use Gmail as a to-do list and content management system. It's where I create certain types of reminders and organize some of my electronic files. Because it uses Google search tools, I use Gmail to store and organize some of my electronic documents too. In this chapter, I'll explain exactly how.

By the way, I'd like to say up front that if you're inclined to skip this chapter because you're tied to using Outlook at work, please stick with me. For one thing, if you work for a company, it's not a great idea to use your work e-mail address for your personal correspondence. You really should have your own separate personal e-mail account, and Gmail is the best option, as I hope you'll soon see.

Plus, if you were laid off, heaven forbid, you might be locked out of your company's e-mail system with little or no warning—meaning you wouldn't be able to take all those personal e-mails with you. So keep your personal e-mail separate from your employer's e-mail account, and make it part of your ever-expanding warehouse of information.

Gmail is also an excellent e-mail aggregator, which makes the service extremely easy to try without repercussions. Let's say you've been using AT&T Yahoo! for your personal e-mail because you get your home DSL service from AT&T. You could set up Gmail to automatically retrieve messages from your AT&T Yahoo! account (and any other e-mail accounts you might have), so you can get all your messages in one place. When you reply to a message within Gmail that it retrieved from your AT&T Yahoo! account, Gmail will automatically put your AT&T Yahoo! address in the "From" field of the message if you so choose. That way, the recipients of your messages won't see that you replied using a new Gmail address, which can cause confusion for them and hassles for you (like explaining to your aunt why you didn't give her your new e-mail address). I'll explain how to use this Gmail feature later in this chapter.

Getting all your e-mail in one place (Gmail) also helps you to be better organized. For one thing, you can search across all your different e-mail accounts quickly and easily. Thus, you're more likely to find a particular message. Secondly, moving all your mail to Gmail allows you to benefit from Gmail's large storage capacity so you can keep all of your messages, essentially, forever.

A Major Innovation

You might be wondering why Google, a company whose sole focus (at least initially) was to offer a search engine, developed an e-mail system in the first place. The answer, you may not be surprised to hear, has to do with search.

Google is a chatty culture. Every day, we'd receive loads of e-mails from colleagues on many different topics. It was extremely difficult to keep all those messages organized. And so a Google engineer came up with Gmail as a way to easily search internal e-mail. The engineer built a prototype of a Web-based, searchable e-mail system and showed it around the company. Other engineers quickly spotted its value. They started using it too, and began adding features to it.

Before long, all sorts of Google employees were using Gmail, which was known back then as 'Caribou.' (This was a reference to the *Dilbert* comic strip and not, sad to say, the Elton John album. But I digress.) More and more Google engineers contributed features to the e-mail system until it became clear we were on to something. And so, Gmail busted out of Google and went public.

When it debuted in 2004, Gmail was a game-changing innovation. Before Gmail, most Web-based e-mail services offered up to about only ten megabytes of storage. That may sound like a lot (and it was, then), but in the world of e-mail storage, ten megabytes fills up very, very quickly, especially if you e-mail large files like PDFs, JPEGs, and MP3s, as so many of us do these days. So this storage ceiling meant you had to frequently delete messages or download them onto your computer to free up new space. Gmail came out of the gate offering an unprecedented (at the time) one gigabyte of online e-mail storage—a ceiling that Google is continually raising. (To compete, other Web-based services have been forced to increase the online storage they offer too.)

I also love that Gmail isn't just about communicating through e-mail. In Gmail, I can send and receive instant messages (IMs). If people you communicate with also use Gmail, you can see their current online status too. So if someone you've been trying to reach is online at the moment, you can send that person a quick IM, sparing you from the tedious back-and-forth of e-mail (or phone calls—only to get the person's voicemail). This helps make communications more immediate, whether it's for business or personal reasons.

Also, I can send a text message directly to someone's cell phone and receive a reply back to my Gmail account. My IMs and text messages become part of my searchable Gmail archive. (When I'm at my computer, I send IMs and text messages whenever possible in Gmail. It's much faster to type them out on a computer keyboard than on my iPhone's on-screen keyboard.) And I can have video chats too. Besides being cool, video chats can make your communications with other people richer because you not only hear what they're saying, you see their reactions. Bottom line: I can do all these things from the same browser page as my Gmail inbox.

Here's one more reason why Gmail is innovative: It takes a different and, in my view, more practical approach to organizing messages—one that runs counter to the often-repeated "Empty your inbox" mantra of organization. Many people feel an empty e-mail inbox gives them a sense of accomplishment. Or, like having an uncluttered desk, it makes them feel less anxious, which allows them to think more clearly. If this approach works for you, great; keep emptying your e-mail inbox. But you don't have to, in order to be organized—thanks to search. You can simply leave everything in your inbox and just search for the e-mails you need when you need them.

I find this method to be far more efficient. After all, think about all the time and effort it takes to maintain an always-empty inbox. To empty your Outlook inbox, you have to either delete messages (a bad idea, in my opinion), or you have to move them into folders. The folder system may be okay if you get only a few e-mails on a very limited number of topics each day. Unfortunately, the world isn't always so simple, or easily compartmentalized. Figuring out where to file each piece of information you receive via e-mail is not only time-consuming and inefficient, it can be close to impossible. Maybe you're collaborating on a project with multiple people. Should you create subfolders to store e-mail from each person you're working with? Maybe you've got a long list of deliverables to complete the project. Should you create folders for each deliverable instead? But there's another problem: Most e-mail systems allow you to file a message in only one folder at a time.

Mother did it need to be so high?

—Pink Floyd, "Mother"

Some of you may be forced to keep your inbox lean. At many companies, users are limited to how much e-mail they can store. This is most common with Outlook/Exchange because e-mail storage systems can be expensive. So users are required to routinely delete or at least archive messages (which puts them in a separate, compressed Outlook file) regularly to free up storage space on the company's e-mail server—yet another step you have to take.

Gmail frees you from worrying about these problems. In Gmail, you don't have to file anything in folders. In fact, Gmail doesn't even have folders. Instead, you leave everything in your inbox. Then you search when you need to find a particular e-mail. And because Gmail stores all your e-mails in the cloud, you can access them from anywhere, anytime.

I just got lost / Every river that I tried to cross.

—Coldplay, "Lost!"

In lieu of folders, Gmail has labels. In a sense, *labels* are like folders in other e-mail programs and services, only they're way better. I create labels in Gmail and apply them either manually or automatically to practically all my e-mail. This allows me to sort and visually scan messages to which I've applied a particular label, and to narrow my e-mail searches. (See the sidebar "Creating Gmail Labels and Filters" for step-by-step instructions on using labels and filters.)

Here's how it works. Let's say I need to find something in an e-mail relating to this book. I may not have a useful keyword in mind to help me search for the message. So I click the Gmail label I created called "Book Stuff" that is automatically applied to all messages sent to or received from my coauthor, Jim, and Talia, our editor.

When I click the "Book Stuff" label, all messages in Gmail with that label are immediately assembled into an orderly list in the inbox, like cadets lining up for a sergeant's inspection. All messages that *aren't* labeled "Book Stuff" are filtered out of view for the moment, so I can concentrate on only the "Book Stuff" messages. Then, by clicking on the "Inbox" link, I can once again see all my Gmail inbox messages, with the most recent ones at the top.

Here's the best part about Gmail: Unlike most e-mail programs that limit you to filing messages in only one folder, I can add multiple labels to any Gmail message. This gives me lots of flexibility for sorting and organizing my e-mail. Example: Most messages relating to this book are labeled "Book Stuff" automatically through the use of Gmail filters I set up. (I'll explain filters and how they work with labels in a minute.) But I can add other labels to those messages too.

I also have a useful (and frequently used) label called "To Do." I apply this label to all sorts of messages—some related to this book, but many not. The common denominator, obviously, is that all the messages labeled "To Do" require me to, well, do something. Thus, when I wanted to quickly see what my to-do items were related to the book, I typed the following in Gmail's search box: *label:book stuff label:to do.* (Do a Google query on *gmail search tips* for ideas on how to quickly find messages in Gmail.) Instantly, Gmail would filter out all messages that aren't labeled "Book Stuff" as well as "To Do." What remained was, in essence, an automatically generated to-do list of items related to this book.

Gmail labels work best when you use them in combination with filters. *Filters* in Gmail are rules that are automatically applied to your e-mail, such as the Gmail filter that automatically applied the "Book Stuff" label to messages from Jim and Talia, as they were received.

Automatically adding labels to messages doesn't mean I'm off the hook for reading those messages, of course. But it helps me prioritize which ones I read, and when I read them. If it weren't for the labels automatically applied to my incoming e-mail, I wouldn't know which messages to read first. I'd be overwhelmed.

To some degree, filtering Gmail messages with labels is akin to filtering textbook chapters the way I did in college. It allows me to focus quickly on what's important so I can ignore, at least for the time being, what isn't. *Gmail filters are the single most important step I've taken to organize the flow of information in my life.* Try it. They take a few minutes to set up, but the payoff is huge.

No matter how you look at it, labels are much more flexible and efficient than folders. Still not convinced? Consider this: If you put a bunch of messages in an Outlook 2007 folder, and you decide later that the folder no longer makes sense, you can rename it. But if you want those messages to be part of your general inbox again, or you want them in another folder, you must literally drag and drop them into their new homes, which can take ages.

With Gmail, however, you can delete or rename labels whenever you want, without affecting the messages bearing those labels. And you don't have to drag messages out of folders because they were never in folders in the first place. Most importantly, it's hard (or impossible) to have a message in two or more folders simultaneously. Gmail allows you to apply as many labels as you want to e-mails, as I described in my discussion about "Book Stuff" and "To Do." Labels give you a flexible system for organizing all your messages, without having to waste the time or brainpower to actually *do* anything to those e-mails.

Let's Talk About Conversations

In addition to labels and filters, Gmail helps me organize my e-mail in other ways too.

If you have a Gmail account (and if you don't, I highly recommend getting one!), you know that Gmail automatically

Gmail's labels and filters are an amazing duo. When used together, you can automatically organize the majority of your incoming e-mail and make messages easier to find down the road. Here's how to do it:

1. Start by creating labels. There are several ways to do this. The easiest is to open an e-mail you'd like to label. Select the "Labels" drop-down menu and then start typing the name of the label you want to create. As you type, Gmail will display the name of the label below where you're typing. Selecting the name as Gmail has displayed it will then create the new label and apply it to that message, all in one step.

   Two things to keep in mind: When you create Gmail labels, try to make them as specific as possible. A "Misc" label, for example, won't really tell you anything about messages labeled as such, other than they're a hodgepodge of stuff (which you already know). Also, you might want to apply second and even third labels to messages because it allows you to group e-mail in more precise and multiple ways.

   One more thing: You can also assign a color to a label, so messages assigned that label will stand out in your crowded Gmail inbox. For instance, I set the "Book Stuff" label so it always appears in red. That way, any e-mails relating to this book automatically grab my attention. To add a color, click the space to the left of a label in your list of labels. This will open a menu of things you can do to that label, such as adding a color. Just don't get too carried away. If all your labels are colored, you've defeated the purpose of coloring them in the first place.

2. Once you have some labels, it's time to start creating your filters. As with generating labels, there's more
   (cont.)

than one way to do this. The simplest is to create a new filter when you have an e-mail open, and you'd like to start filtering future messages similar in some way to that message. For instance, you're reading an e-mail from your friend Nick and you want to automatically apply your "Friends" label to all messages Nick sends you. To do this, you'd select the "More actions" drop-down menu when a message from Nick is open; then you'd click "Filter messages like these." You can add other criteria to the filter too, such as specific words. Then, click the "Next Step" button. This is where you put a check mark next to "Apply the label:" and then select from a drop-down menu the label you want to automatically apply to all messages from Nick (you can also add new labels to this menu anytime). Gmail gives you the option to retroactively apply the label to the messages you've already received from Nick, as well as to future e-mails. When you're finished, click "Create Filter," and you're done.

Please note that these steps, as with others described in this book, were accurate at the time I wrote this. Technology being technology, it's possible they may be slightly different by the time you read this. By the way, check out my blog at douglascmerrill.com, where I'll update you on cool tools for organization, plus offer additional tips and strategies for being organized in the twenty-first century.

threads, or groups, related messages into *conversations.* Each e-mail and the subsequent responses to it are organized chronologically in a continual conversation thread, with the most recent message at the bottom. If you sent me a message, and I replied to it, and you replied to my response, those three messages would be grouped together in Gmail as one conversation. This means that by default, Gmail adds context to all my messages (and by now, you know how important context is to me), allowing me to quickly see how an e-mail exchange evolved, who participated, and what was said most recently on the subject.

Let me give you an example to show you what a time-saver this can be. If I've been out of the loop for some reason, when I'm back online, I may find multiple e-mails on a particular subject. Rather than reading every one, trying to determine what action, if any, I should take, I'll just scroll down to the most recent message in the thread. This usually tells me what I need to know, or at least, what the latest thinking is on a given topic. And this way, if someone has already taken action on the matter, I'll see it right away and not waste time duplicating anyone's efforts. If I'm not sure what I'm supposed to do, I can jump back to the beginning or middle of the thread to figure it out, without having to sort through a million different messages.

E-mail conversations also help ensure that you never respond to the wrong e-mail. Let's say you were out of the office for an hour or so, without e-mail access. When you return, you find a request for information that your boss sent to you and several of your colleagues. As soon as you read the message, you respond with an answer. And then, whoops, you discover by scrolling further through your inbox that someone else had already answered the question and cc-ed you. Suddenly, instead of looking responsive, you look redundant. Plus, you've wasted time and energy looking up or trying to remember the relevant information and crafting a response that wasn't necessary. But with Gmail, you'd have seen any replies to your boss's query *before* you responded. I can't tell you how many times this has spared me embarrassment.

Adding a Plus Sign to Your Gmail Address

Another cool organizing feature in Gmail I use often is the + sign in e-mail addresses. By adding the + sign to your Gmail address when you give it to someone, you can automatically filter messages that aren't necessarily spam but are hard to filter because they may come from various e-mail addresses.

Let's consider online shopping. Each site you buy from wants your e-mail address to send you a receipt, notify you of shipment, and so on. But you can bet they'll also use your e-mail address to send you e-coupons, information about future offers, and spam until the end of time. Because future messages from these sites may have important information regarding your purchases, adding these sites to your spam filter isn't a good solution. Plus, they may come from multiple addresses (all generated by the same site, of course) that are hard to predict and apply filters to. On the other hand, you don't want a bunch of junk e-mail from e-commerce sites filling up your inbox either.

You have options. You could create an e-mail address for each of the companies from which you buy online. This is messy, inefficient, and uses up addresses that others might want. And you don't need to do it. All you need is a + in Gmail.

Here's what you'd do: If your Gmail address is *yourname@gmail.com*, you give your address to each e-commerce site you buy from as *yourname+shopping@gmail.com*. You don't have to set up a new Gmail account for that e-mail address. Just add the + sign between your e-mail ID and *@gmail.com*.

> **Is to have had and lost / Better than not having at all?**
> —Coldplay featuring Jay-Z, "Lost+"

Next, you could set up a Gmail filter that would automatically archive all incoming messages addressed to *yourname+shopping@gmail.com*. By doing this, you'd automatically push messages from all e-commerce sites out of your active inbox and into your Gmail archive. As a result, those messages wouldn't distract or irritate you because they'd be out of view. However, they'd still be available through a search or by viewing your Inbox. Alternatively, you could create a filter that automatically adds a label, such as "Shopping," to any message sent to *yourname+shopping@gmail.com*. Then you could view and sort all messages related to your e-commerce activities if you wanted.

What's the point of all this? It's an easy, automated way to organize e-mail you may or may not want to read. The +

sign essentially gives you an automatic filter that's instantly applied to all e-mails about online shopping, and all you had to do was set up that one filter.

To-Do Lists and Other Gmail Uses

Beyond e-mail, here are some other ways I use Gmail.

TO KEEP TRACK OF TO-DOS

Often, an e-mail is really just a new to-do item traveling incognito. "Please read the attached presentation and give me your comments asap." "Please sign and fax back the attached invoice." Or everyone's favorite: "Please respond to this message so we can transfer one million dollars to your bank account."

Every day, I receive dozens of e-mails that require me to take action. To create a quick visual reminder for myself as I'm reading a message, I click an icon in Gmail to add a yellow star next to the e-mail. The star is a visual cue that I need to follow up on the message.

Later, I can click "Starred" in Gmail and immediately see only those messages to which I've added a yellow star. It's the same principle as a Gmail label. All the messages without a star are instantly filtered out of view for the moment. What remains is like an instant to-do list of starred messages. I didn't have to manually add items to a to-do list. I didn't have to remember which messages needed follow-up. Gmail does both for me. At least once a day, I review all my starred Gmail messages, to make sure I've followed up on them. Once I have, I remove the star.

Adding stars to Gmail messages is similar to the "flag" function in Outlook. Both serve to add visual reminders to follow up on an e-mail. Clicking the flag icon on your Outlook menu puts all of your flagged e-mail at the top of your inbox, with all other messages falling below. But it's not as effective because it doesn't hide the nonflagged items from view. And I'm more productive when I can visually filter out everything that's not important, so I can focus on what is.

There are other ways to visually flag Gmail messages for follow-up. But starring them, in my opinion, is the easiest and best method because it requires me to take only one step—clicking the star icon next to the e-mail.

TO SEND REMINDERS TO MYSELF AND OTHERS

Sometimes I send messages to my Gmail address to serve as reminders for things that aren't especially time sensitive. They're usually just things that need a bit of context, such as a Web link or an attached document.

For example, in the previous chapter, I mentioned that when I receive an important paper document, such as a contract, I request a PDF copy of it or scan it myself. Then I send a message to my own Gmail account. In the message I include a reminder of where I filed the original paper document. I'll also add a few keywords to the message, to ensure that I'll find the e-mail easily in a search.

This is critical, by the way, and in fact it's my eighteenth principle of organization: *Add relevant keywords to your digital information so you can easily find it later.*

> Add relevant keywords to your digital information so you can easily find it later.

Finally, I attach the PDF of the original document, copy Sonya, and hit "Send." The message and the document then become part of my searchable Gmail archive, which I can now access from my phone or any computer.

Similarly, when I register a new user ID and password to a Web site, I send an e-mail reminder to my Gmail account. The message includes the site's URL, along with my user ID and a password hint. I label each of these messages "Credentials," so I can quickly sort them in Gmail as needed. (See the sidebar in this chapter "Organizing Your Passwords" for ideas about making your passwords more secure.)

Gmail has a Contacts utility that automatically creates an address book for you, based on people you send to and receive e-mail from. You can also import your address book from Outlook, Yahoo!, and other places, or create new contact entries.

The Gmail Contacts is certainly convenient. If you start to type in an address in the "To" line of a new message, and that person is in your Gmail address book, Gmail will automatically finish typing the e-mail address for you.

But as address books go, Gmail's Contacts utility is fairly basic. I use it primarily to store the e-mail addresses of people with whom I correspond, since it captures those addresses automatically when I respond to a message. But I keep my address book in Apple's MobileMe service, because it offers more features than Gmail's Contacts. I make all my address book changes directly in MobileMe. In turn, those changes are automatically pushed to the address book on my Mac and on my iPhone. Also, I prefer using MobileMe because the interface is remarkably easy. I can enter data on the Web or into my address book directly, and the synchronization between MobileMe, my iPhone, and my MacBook Air is reasonably reliable. Taken together, these two factors give me a preference for MobileMe.

Earlier in this chapter, I pointed out the importance of using the tools you already have, whenever possible, instead of adding new ones. But it's equally important to use the right tool for each system you build for organizing information. As you can see, sometimes these two principles clash. When that happens, you have to remember your goals. In this particular case, my goals are to have a centrally stored address book that's consistent across all my devices and that's easy to update on any of my devices. Because of those goals, I decided to use the best tool for the job, MobileMe, rather than a tool I already had (Gmail's Contacts).

147

Living with Outlook E-Mail

By now you get the general idea: I strongly prefer Gmail to Outlook. (As of this writing, I have not had the opportunity to try Outlook 2010, so my comments are related to Outlook 2007 and earlier versions.) But if you're still using Outlook for your work e-mail (indeed, most companies still require you use it), there are ways to add some Gmail-like touches to Microsoft Outlook and to organize your Outlook e-mail more efficiently. (You can install a number of add-on utilities that make Outlook a more hospitable place to live. See the "Stuff We Love" appendix for ideas.)

For example, as I mentioned earlier, you can use Outlook flags the way you'd use Gmail's stars. In fact, Outlook flags have an additional feature that can be very useful. By right-clicking on a message and selecting "Follow up" in the pop-up menu, then "Add reminder," you can set a to-do item with a reminder that will pop up later on your computer screen and/or your phone. This can be a great way to keep track of tasks or items that need to be completed by a certain date. (By the way, Gmail has a Tasks tool too. It lets you create a new task from any e-mail, or create tasks independently of your messages. You can then assign a date on your Google Calendar to each task.)

The "Arrange by Conversation" option in Outlook 2007 is roughly similar in concept to Gmail's conversation threads. (Outlook 2010 offers improved conversation views. Other programs that provide conversation views include Mozilla's Thunderbird at mozillamessaging.com and Zoho's cloud e-mail service at zoho.com.) To give it a try in Outlook 2007, go to "View" (on the top menu bar), then select "Arrange by" and then "Conversation." Outlook will then group multiple messages on the same topic together. But Gmail still gets my vote for providing the simplest and cleanest conversation view.

Outlook 2007 offers some features that at least approximate the usefulness of Gmail labels. You can create a color-coded category and automatically apply it to e-mail from a specific person or on a certain topic and then sort your mes-

As I mentioned earlier in this chapter, Gmail does a terrific job of fetching e-mail from multiple e-mail accounts. This makes it easy to corral all your various e-mail accounts into one inbox in Gmail; send messages using your other e-mail addresses (making it easy to try Gmail out without confusing the people you correspond with or requiring them to update your e-mail address in their address books); and leave copies of all messages forwarded to Gmail on your other e-mail account servers. This lets you continue to use your other e-mail service if you want, while you decide if Gmail is for you or not.

To pull e-mail from other accounts into your Gmail, go to "Settings," then click "Accounts and Import." Under "Check mail using, POP3," click the "Add POP3 e-mail account" button. Next, type in the e-mail address, and click the "Next Step" button. Enter the user name and password to your e-mail account. If you want, check the box next to "Leave a copy of retrieved message on the server." You may also need to check "Always use a secure connection (SSL) when retrieving mail," depending on the security requirements of your Internet service provider (ISP). Click "Add account" to finish the job.

sages by those categories—but the process is extremely complicated. First you have to select and name a category and assign it a color. Then you have to create a rule, select the conditions for the rule, edit the rule description, then choose all the contacts for whom the rule should apply. *Then* you have to select any exceptions to that rule, give the rule a name, and lastly, turn it on. As I said, it's convoluted. You can see why I think Gmail's labels feature beats Outlook's categories for sheer simplicity and ease of use.

What's Stopping You?

Even if your company insists you use Outlook for your work e-mail, I still recommend using Gmail for your personal e-mail.

Gmail is a nearly ideal scaffold for organizing all the information of your personal and work life. It's easy to use, and it has virtually unlimited storage. Gmail allows you to search years of messages quickly. It can organize lots of different types of information—including tasks, random bits of data gathered online, important documents, and contacts—so you can access that information at any time. And the Gmail page is neat and clean, which appeals to my interface preferences. The ads are unobtrusive, which helps you stay mentally focused on the information and tasks at hand. You can try it without even having to change your e-mail address. Gmail lets you consolidate multiple e-mail accounts easily into one account too. And it's free, so what's stopping you?

ENCODE THIS

- A scaffold is a digital tool for storing, organizing, and searching digital information. Gmail comes closest to being an ideal scaffold. It's free, easy to use, and offers tons of storage.

- In lieu of folders, Gmail uses labels, which are more efficient and flexible. You can apply multiple labels to one message and then filter your messages according to their assigned labels. You can't do that with folders.

- Gmail adds context to all messages because it groups them into conversations. This allows you to quickly see how an e-mail exchange evolved, who participated, and what was said most recently on the subject.

- By adding the + sign to your Gmail address and giving that address only to certain senders, you can automatically filter messages from those senders.

Living in the twenty-first century, you've probably accumulated dozens of user IDs and passwords to frequently visited sites. It's critical to choose safe passwords, to protect your personal information from identity thieves and hackers. However, choosing good passwords isn't always enough. To be really secure, you should change your passwords at least every six months (and when I say "changing them," I mean *really* changing them—not just tacking on a number at the beginning or end). Also, don't repeat any passwords. Each site you use should have a unique password. This way, if one password somehow gets stolen or compromised, you don't have to worry about all the others.

But if we all have a million long, complicated passwords that are always changing, how can we possibly be expected to store and keep track of them safely?

There are plenty of software utilities and browser tools dedicated just to this task. But why learn or buy another tool when you can use one you already know? Gmail is really all you need to store this sensitive information—as long as you're smart about how you do it. I use Gmail to store a list of user IDs and password *clues* that only I can easily decipher. I don't recommend writing down exact passwords in Gmail or anywhere else. Instead, I give myself enough of a hint so my brain can figure out the rest.

Example: In an e-mail reminder for a new password to an eBay account, I might write something like "first four letters of spouse's hometown + Mom's birthday + last six letters of my least favorite city." Because these have meaning for me, when prompted with these clues I don't have to expend extra brainpower trying to remember them. And yet, my passwords are still safe because they're specific enough to me that no one else (except maybe Sonya) will be able to crack them.

The worst passwords are single words like "Tyrone,"

(cont.)

when everyone knows that's your dog's name. The best ones are reasonably long combinations of numbers and letters that don't make a word at all. Random strings of numbers and letters, however, are impossible to remember, which is why I have a system.

Start by taking a phrase you'll remember, like a favorite song lyric. Then, take the first letter of each word in the lyric, and make every other letter a capital letter and the rest in lowercase. *Voilà!* You have a strong password.

For example, let's pretend your favorite artist is Pink Floyd. (If not, Pink Floyd should be in your top ten. Really, trust me.) And it might turn out that you particularly love their masterpiece *The Wall.* You could create a strong password built on the phrase *Pink Floyd Another Brick in the Wall,* combining the band with the title of their well-known song from *The Wall.* (I used to create passwords based entirely on Stevie Nicks songs, but I've moved on.)

Start by taking the first letter of each word of your phrase, which would give you *PFABITW.* Then you could make the password even stronger by adding punctuation, such as *PFABITW!* Next, you could alternately change the case of the letters, which would give you *PfAbItW!* If you don't feel that this password is secure enough, you could add numerals to the password, such as the date you and your spouse met. If that were June 3, 1998, your password would then be *PfAbItW!06031998.* You've now created an extremely strong password that would be hard for someone (or an automated tool designed to crack passwords) to figure out.

Then send yourself a Gmail with a clue that will jog your memory, such as: favorite band, favorite song from that band's best album, alternate caps and lowercase, add an exclamation point, plus the month, day, and year I met my spouse. Yes, it's a lot of work, and frankly, it's probably overkill. But you get the idea, and you can (and should) adapt it to what's comfortable for you. When it comes to securing your personal information, my philosophy is better safe than sorry, but you don't want to set the security bar so high that you end up not following your own rules.

Remember, even if you have the kinds of passwords that would make a CIA operative proud, you still have to be careful with them. For example, don't leave your e-mail application or e-mail service open to anyone who might pass by your desk while you're off getting your third cappuccino. Ideally, you should always log out of e-mail when you'll be away from your computer. This can be a bit of a pain, of course. An easier option: Set up your computer so that it goes into sleep mode after, say, 15 minutes of disuse. Then require a password to wake it up from screen saver mode or from sleep.

- Gmail's star feature adds a visual cue to messages that require action. Viewing only your starred messages gives you what is essentially an updated to-do list.

- At least once a day, review your starred Gmail messages to make sure you've followed up as needed.

- You can also use Gmail to send yourself and others reminders and to store and search for backups of documents.

- Whenever possible, use tools you already know, rather than investing time and money in new ones.

- Store password hints (but not the actual passwords) in a place that's easy for you to access (that is, in the cloud), like your Gmail account.

chapter 10

THANKS FOR SHARING

why you should keep your
calendar in the cloud

Y LIFE, LIKE YOURS, is a fairly complicated mix of professional and personal stuff. One is always overlapping the other. I take care of business at night and on weekends; I do personal stuff sometimes during the workday. So why should I organize my calendar (a.k.a., my life) based on which appointments are work related and which ones aren't? How does that help me be organized?

> So much time to make up...time we have wasted on the way.
>
> —Crosby, Stills, & Nash, "Wasted on the Way"

It doesn't. And that's why the Microsoft Outlook/Exchange model, so widely used in the corporate world, is fundamentally wrong for what we need today.

Though it has e-mail and other capabilities, Outlook/Exchange is essentially an office calendar system for company employees. As such, it builds a fortified castle around your work calendar. You can share it with people inside the castle, but there's no drawbridge to let the villagers in. Okay, as you can see, I played *Dungeons and Dragons* one too many times in my misspent youth. Translation: Your Outlook/Exchange calendar isn't designed to be shared with anyone outside an organization. (The same is true if you use Outlook as a personal calendaring program on your home computer.)

I realize there are valid reasons for doing things the Outlook/Exchange way. Companies want to keep their information private as much as possible, for starters. But this is a calendar system designed around an outdated, unhelpful assumption that work and life are two separate worlds. A better approach, in my mind, is a calendar system built to be shared with whomever you want, whenever you want. One that's always available and always the same, regardless of the device you view it on. One that you can search easily and thoroughly. And one that keeps track of your *entire* life, not just certain segments of it.

Google's online calendaring system, Google Calendar (google.com/calendar), accomplishes all the above. This chapter is about how I use GCal, which is one of my most important scaffolds, to organize my calendar and my life.

A Calendar to Search and Share

While I believe it's ideal to use one calendaring system like GCal for all your appointments, I also realize you may have no choice but to use Outlook/Exchange for your work calendar. If that's the case, I recommend that you keep your personal calendar appointments in GCal anyway, for the same reason I advocated using Gmail as your personal e-mail in chapter 9—you should think of your calendar appointments as part of your own personal searchable database. Yes, this means you'll need to maintain at least two calendars, one in Outlook/Exchange and one in GCal, which can add complexity to your life and possibly introduce errors if you're not vigilant. Alas, we live in an imperfect world, and I think this hassle can be worth the pain, ultimately. And there is hope: You could suggest, ever so politely, that your IT folks consider moving the whole company to Google Apps (which includes GCal). Give them this link, http://www.google.com/apps/intl/en/business/, and perhaps some fresh-baked cookies to get them motivated.

By the way, there are various tools such as Google Calendar Sync (to find it, search for *google calendar sync*) that automatically sync Outlook and GCal calendars. Synchronizations in general can be tricky, and in the case of Google Calendar Sync, your computer must have an active Internet connection for the sync to work. Still, Google Calendar Sync or a tool like it might be worth trying if you're wedded to Outlook for whatever reason but you'd like to use GCal too.

GCal works pretty much like the calendar in Outlook and other programs. You add appointments or you accept appointment invitations from other people, which are then automatically added to your calendar. To create a new GCal appointment, you can click the "Quick Add" link (under the Google Calendar logo) or hit *Q* on your keyboard while in GCal. Then type something like, "Dinner with Sonya, Friday, 7 P.M.," and GCal will add the appointment to your calendar for the appropriate time and day. If you need to add more detail to an appointment, you select "Create Event" under the GCal logo to begin your new calendar entry.

But GCal has some useful features not all other calendar systems offer.

Like Gmail, GCal is extremely easy to search, and searches are fast and thorough. You just type your keyword or phrase in the blank search field and click the "Search My Calendars" button. Advanced search options let you search a specific calendar, or all of them; search by dates, locations, people, and subjects; and exclude calendar items with certain words. You'll find the advanced search operators by clicking the "Show Search Options" link in GCal.

I also love the abilities to set up multiple appointment alerts (one alert isn't always enough) and to receive alerts in a variety of ways—as pop-up reminders, e-mail messages, and/or text messages. My favorite is to have reminders sent as text messages to my iPhone because that's the one device

I almost always carry with me. You can specify how and when you receive reminders when setting up a new calendar entry. Currently, GCal can nudge you up to five different times for a single event.

Then there are the many small but incredibly useful touches GCal offers. You can get the weather forecast built right into your calendar view, so you'll know if you need to wear a raincoat to the Lollapalooza. To add weather, click "Settings," "General," enter your ZIP code or city for "Location," and then choose °C or °F. The forecast will come up as a small icon (such as a sun with or without clouds) for each day it's available. Put your cursor over the icon, and you'll see what the projected high and low temperatures are.

You can also use GCal as an event announcement or invitation service, like Evite.com. When you set up a new GCal event, there's a box to the right for adding guests (by adding their e-mail addresses, separated by commas). GCal will track who has responded, how many people are coming to the event, and so on.

One of the most useful features of GCal, though, is that it makes it easy to share your calendars with other people.

Sonya and I maintain multiple GCal calendars, and we share each one of them with a specific person or set of people. By "share," I mean that I can give others the ability to view one of my GCal calendars using their own computer's Web browser, even if they don't also use GCal. If they do use GCal, they can see my appointments alongside their own. In addition to viewing privileges, I can give others the right to add, change, or delete my GCal appointments.

I keep one GCal calendar specifically for business travel and other business-related appointments. I share this calendar with my assistant, who enters the appointments, and Sonya. Given my hectic travel schedule, Sonya needs to know when I'll be in town before getting tickets to a show, agreeing to a dinner party invitation, or whatever. It's not always easy for her to reach me when she needs to, so giving her online access to my calendar makes scheduling joint activities so much easier.

Sonya keeps her work schedule in a separate GCal calendar, which she shares with me and some of her colleagues. In addition, we share a joint GCal calendar for the concerts, parties, vacations, and other activities we do together. We keep yet another GCal calendar that contains our travel schedule and other appointments. We share this calendar with people who are affected by it, such as our dog walker. At this point you might be thinking, "I thought you said it was a bad idea to try to separate personal and work calendars"? It is. The beauty of GCal is that it allows us to view these separate calendars as one giant, searchable, filterable, color-coded, *organized* calendar.

ORGANIZING TO-DOS

You can create lists of tasks in GCal (and Gmail), Outlook, iCal, and other calendaring programs. But managing and organizing to-dos aren't necessarily a calendar program's forte. So I've opted to use a program called Things (culturedcode.com/things), which is dedicated just to handling to-do items.

Things is an app for iPhones and Macs, and it does a great job synchronizing my tasks between the two. Most importantly, Things gives me lots of ways to organize my to-do items. I can maintain multiple to-do lists; group them into projects; assign deadlines to them or just drop them into the "Someday" category; and add searchable tags to each to-do item.

As I've mentioned before, I always try to use the tools I already have and know, and that require the least amount of work for the job at hand. That's why, when I'm in Gmail, I star or slap a "To Do" label on e-mail that requires me to take some action. But for all my other to-do items, I need a tool that has much more robust organizing capabilities and that I can take with me wherever I go. That tool is Things.

Red = Work, Blue = Fun

Maintaining multiple calendars in GCal might seem confusing or difficult. But in reality, it's much simpler than it sounds.

For one thing, GCal makes it fairly easy to copy an appointment from one calendar to another. When you create a new appointment, you can designate only one calendar. But after you create it, you can open that appointment, click the "More Actions" drop-down menu in GCal, and select "Copy to…," choosing the calendar to which you want to copy the appointment. Click "Save" to finish the copying. You'll need to manually repeat the action for each calendar, but the whole process takes just a few seconds.

Also, I can see all the appointments from all my calendars in one single GCal calendar view, with each appointment color-coded so I can tell which calendar it belongs to. For instance, my GCal work appointments are red, the appointments from our joint calendar are blue, and Sonya's work appointments are green. So when I view all of our calendars combined into one GCal view, I can tell at a glance which appointments are for my work, which ones are for Sonya's work, and so on. I can add or remove a calendar from the combined calendar view just by clicking the name of the calendar.

By now, you might be wondering, "If all the information shows up on one big calendar anyway, what are the benefits (besides making life a little easier for the dog walker) of having separate calendars?" To answer that excellent question, let me remind you of the theme of chapter 7. To me, sharing specific calendars with specific people makes a lot of sense from a *filtering* perspective.

For example, our dog walker doesn't need to know the details of my work schedule or our social calendar. But if Sonya and I simply maintained one massive calendar between the two of us and shared it with our dog walker, she'd quickly be overwhelmed. She wouldn't be able to easily see only those things that matter to her. And so, giving her access to one mega calendar would actually be counterproductive.

By sharing a calendar with our dog walker that only contains the appointments that affect her, Sonya and I are, in effect, filtering our calendars for her. This serves our primary goal of sharing a calendar with our dog walker in the first place: to make it easy for her to know when she's needed.

Sharing a calendar also minimizes the back-and-forth in e-mail and phone calls that often occurs when you're trying to coordinate your calendar with others' schedules. More importantly, though, I can easily filter out of view calendars I'm not interested in seeing at the moment. If I need to concentrate only on my work appointments, I won't get distracted by our social schedule or Sonya's work calendar. This ability to filter out things I don't need to see at a given point in time is incredibly important in keeping my mind focused. As you'll remember from chapter 1, the brain is good at attending to only a certain number of things at once, and it can be easily overwhelmed by the jam-packed schedule of two busy people. That said, if I do need to see everything all at once, I can.

For instance, if I were to plan a surprise birthday party for Sonya (surprise, honey!), I'd have to make sure I'll be in town on the night I'm planning for, she doesn't have to work the next day, we don't already have plans that night, and so on. I can figure this out quickly by viewing all our calendars at once.

GCal is an efficient way to coordinate activities that include a lot of people, like team or group events. Your kid's soccer team could post its game schedule in a shared GCal calendar. If you're a GCal user, you could then add that calendar to your set of GCal calendars so that all the games would show up on your master GCal view. And even if you don't use GCal (although I hope by now you're at least considering it), you can just follow a Web link to view the calendar in your browser.

GCal isn't the only cloud calendar system, of course. For example, MobileMe, which I discussed in chapter 9, has a calendar component. I'm not knocking MobileMe's calendar. It does a good job of automatically syncing appointments between MobileMe in the cloud, desktop calendar programs

My typical workday is full of meetings and appointments. In the span of just a few hours, I may have to jump from a videoconference about some technology issue to a budget meeting to a meeting with a direct report. In the worst-case scenario, I find myself going into the next meeting asking, "Remind me what this is about?"

To prevent that from happening, I make sure all my calendar entries include some context. When my assistant adds a new meeting to my calendar, she types notes directly into the appointment entry, telling me things like the topic and goals of the meeting and who the other participants will be. If I don't know one of the attendees, my assistant may add a few notes about that person, such as a job title, what he or she is contributing to the project at hand, and so on.

Similarly, I add bits of context whenever possible to my address book entries. If you and I just met and might be working together in the future, I'd add a note of who introduced us or where we met in my address book entry for you. I might also add your spouse's name, your birthday, or anything else that might be important to remember about you. If I thought I'd be visiting you later, I'd include a Google Maps link in your address book entry for driving directions to your home or office.

161

(including iCal on Macs and Outlook on Windows), and the calendar programs on iPhones and iPod Touch players.

And you can create and maintain multiple MobileMe calendars. For instance, using MobileMe within your Web browser, you'd click the plus sign in the bottom left-hand corner of the screen, select "New calendar," then give the calendar a name and assign a color to it. MobileMe also lets you group calendars. You could maintain separate calendars for, say, your book group meetings and your volleyball team's games, then group them into one calendar category called

"Activities." This gives you the option to make both those calendars invisible or visible on your combined MobileMe calendar view with one click. (You turn a calendar on or off by clicking the checkbox next to the name of the calendar or calendar group.) You also have the option of turning on or off each calendar individually within a calendar group.

> One minute I held the key /
> Next the walls were closed on me.
> —Coldplay, "Viva La Vida"

That said, unlike GCal, MobileMe calendars aren't designed to be shared with others. And as of this writing, Apple doesn't offer a way to search your MobileMe calendars from within a Web browser. While MobileMe is a solid service in many ways, when it comes to calendaring, GCal meets my goals best because it's extremely easy to search and share.

ENCODE THIS

- The Microsoft Outlook/Exchange puts a barrier between work and personal appointments, which is at odds with how we live and doesn't help us be organized.

- A better solution is to keep multiple calendars in the cloud and then share each calendar with the people most likely to be affected by it. GCal makes this easy.

- GCal is extremely easy to search. Searches are fast and thorough. And GCal is free.

- The people you share your GCal calendars with don't have to be GCal users. To see your calendar, all they need is a browser and an Internet connection.

- By sharing specific calendars with specific people, you're filtering your schedule for them.

- Sharing a calendar also reduces the back-and-forth that occurs when you're trying to coordinate your schedule with others.

chapter 11

A BROWSER, AN OPERATING SYSTEM & SOME COOL STICKERS

organizing your documents and web content

SO FAR, I'VE COVERED a lot of the information we deal with nearly every day: snail mail and paper documents; e-mail, instant messages, and text messages; address books; calendar appointments and to-do lists. This chapter is about the other important digital information in our lives—documents (such as text files) and Web content—and the scaffolds I use to manage them.

Let's start with documents. Most of us are used to creating a document, like a Microsoft Word file, and then e-mailing it to others for their input. But through this process errors can be introduced. And it's difficult to track all the various versions floating around. Then there's the added burden of keeping all your documents backed up somehow.

Instead, I create and store many of my personal documents using Google Docs. With Google Docs (docs.google.com), you don't buy or install any software, as you do with Microsoft Office. Instead, you can do everything right in your Web browser. You can upload documents you've already created in Word or another program. (See the sidebar "Getting Started with Google Docs" in this chapter for how-to instructions.) Or you can generate new files (text, spreadsheets, presentations, and forms) directly in Google Docs.

I can see my Google Docs files from any computer or phone browser. Better yet, I don't even have to be online because Google Docs has an offline mode too. And my Google Docs files are magically backed up. This is important: If my laptop goes missing (as it did at airport security not long ago), at least my Google Docs files are safe because they live in the cloud, not on my computer. In fact, my goal is to not keep much on my laptop aside from a Web browser, an operating system, and a few cool stickers.

Google Docs serves my goal of collaborating with others on basic documents particularly well. For example, not long ago, Sonya and I completed a massive home renovation, and Google Docs helped us throughout the project.

Once we'd decided to move from the Bay Area to Los Angeles, we found a house we loved in Hollywood. It was built in the 1930s for none other than Bela Lugosi, the actor who'd become famous for playing Dracula. The house had great "bones" (pun somewhat intended), but it had fallen into disrepair over the years. Interestingly enough, Lugosi didn't add any bizarre touches to the house. It was a subsequent owner who, knowing the house's history, added gargoyles and various other creepy-castle flourishes. But I digress.

So, on top of all the other changes in our lives Sonya and I were experiencing at the time, we somehow also needed to manage a major home renovation. Like any huge project, a home renovation involves organizing and sharing lots of information. Here are the ways we used Google Docs to achieve this:

To store important documents. Our home renovation project required obtaining various inspections before some of the work could be performed. Most inspection reports came to us as PDFs, which I would upload to Google Docs. That way, all the reports were in one place, which we could both access from anywhere, and Sonya and I didn't have to worry about not being able to find an inspector's report on, say, the chimney, or other part of the house, when we needed it.

To keep a master to-do list. Sonya and I made a master Google Docs spreadsheet of all the work that needed to be done. Either one of us could add to this spreadsheet from our computers or from our iPhones, which was helpful, given that I was in London a lot during the renovations. We'd use this spreadsheet to track what we wanted to do, and then to note what had been done and when. In some cases, I'd write in the spreadsheet that something had been completed, but Sonya didn't agree that the job was done to satisfaction and she would edit the document to mark the item as incomplete. This system helped us minimize the inevitable confusion and stress that's typical of so many major home renovations.

To keep track of the money. We received bids from multiple contractors and subcontractors for various jobs throughout the house. Sonya and I needed to keep records of those bids in a way that would make them easily accessible to us both. So we built a separate spreadsheet in Google Docs that focused specifically on contractors and money. In this spreadsheet, we listed all the various contractors and subcontractors we'd hired, the work each one was doing, when they'd been paid and how much, and so on. We'd use the graph feature in Google Docs to get a quick visualization of how much we'd spent at any given time during the project.

All told, thanks to tools like Google Docs, computers, and iPhones, we managed to finish a huge home renovation project within about twelve months. All that was left to do was relax, have a cup of tea, and watch an old movie classic. You know, something like *Bela Lugosi Meets a Brooklyn Gorilla*.

Real-Time Collaboration

Taking notes in meetings is another way I use Google Docs as a collaborative tool.

I often find myself in the position of taking notes in meetings that will be sent out as minutes later. However, sending them out later isn't ideal, since it's hard to make changes after the notes have been distributed. And so, during meetings, I frequently type notes on my laptop into a Google Docs text file, and I give editing access to the document to everyone participating in the meeting. (You can give people view-only access to a Google Docs file or allow them to edit the file too. I'll explain how to do this in the "Getting Started with Google Docs" sidebar.) I also connect my laptop to the company's network and to a conference room projector, when one's available. This accomplishes a number of things: Everyone participating in the meeting can see my notes as I type them—including those who are physically present but didn't bring a laptop (they see the notes on the projection screen) and remote attendees, who can follow the notes as they're created on their computers at home. Also, everyone in the meeting with a laptop and those participating remotely can add their own notes to the same document I'm typing in.

> I got no time for private consultation.
>
> —The Church, "Under the Milky Way"

Inevitably, someone will read my notes during the meeting and say, "I know that's what I said, but what I *meant* was…" No problem; typing the notes in real time in Google Docs allows us to correct the notes on the spot. My system also helps people participating remotely to better understand what's going on. In the conference room, someone may be moving around, shuffling papers, or talking softly, making it difficult for anyone listening in by speakerphone to hear what's being said. But when remote attendees follow the meeting notes on their computer screens, if they miss something, they can read my notes to catch up or get clarification.

And so, what was once a solitary endeavor—me scribbling meeting notes on paper—has evolved into a real-time collaboration. My notes are no longer just what I got out of what was said; together, everyone in a meeting creates a richer historical record of that session, with better context and a broader range of knowledge and perspectives. The notes we capture can drive deeper, more productive discussions later. And they give those who weren't there a better understanding of who said what during the meeting.

The biggest downside to Google Docs is that it doesn't have anywhere near the features you'd get with Microsoft Office applications like Word, Excel, or PowerPoint.

For example, when writing this book, Jim and I could have used Google Docs. Early on, we tried to do so. But it's not really set up to deal with long, complex, footnoted prose, which is why Jim and I didn't use it when writing this book (if we had, I would have avoided the hassles of version control and of making sure I had the right file on my laptop when I needed it). Google Docs is much better suited for simpler documents where real-time collaboration is a key goal, such as meeting notes.

For more complicated documents, I find it much easier to craft my prose in a full-featured word processor like Microsoft Word (which, unlike Google Docs, allows me to use the helpful Track Changes feature) and then e-mail those files to myself, as well as to anyone else who might need them. By e-mailing the file to my Gmail account, I ensure that the file attachment will be stored in the cloud, as well as on my hard drive. And as long as I give the file a good, descriptive label, *including the date it was last updated,* that file will be easy to search for and locate when I need it later.

Organizing the Ephemeral

As you can see, Google Docs is useful for developing content through easy, real-time collaboration. But what about all the Web content relevant to your life that *other people* create, like news stories, product reviews, and blog posts? How do

GETTING STARTED WITH GOOGLE DOCS

Anyone with a free Google account can use Google Docs. Start by going to docs.google.com and either sign in using your Gmail address and password or create a new Google account. When you're signed into Gmail, you can click on the "Documents" link in the upper left corner of the browser page displaying your inbox.

Are you in Google Docs now? Cool. Here are a few things to get you going.

1. To start a new document, click "Create new" drop-down menu, and select "Document," "Presentation," "Spreadsheet," "Form," or "Folder." Give your new file a name by clicking "Untitled" (or a variation thereof) above the document and start typing in the new file name. (The program will automatically and frequently save your new file.) Click "OK" when you're finished naming the document.

2. When you're done working on your file, you can hit "Share," "Save," or "Save & Close." In the "Share" drop-down menu, you can send e-mails inviting others to be collaborators (giving them editing privileges) on the document. Or you can invite them as viewers (which doesn't give them the ability to edit). Other options include e-mailing the document directly to someone as an attachment or publishing the file as a public Web page.

3. Alternatively, you can upload files you've already created on your computer. At the moment, supported file formats include Microsoft Word (doc, docx), rich text format (rtf), Microsoft PowerPoint (ppt, pps), Microsoft Excel (xls, xlsx), and PDF (pdf). Once you've uploaded your files, you can share them for real-time collaboration, just as you could any other Google Docs file.

you capture the information you find online that you might need later?

Most people will bookmark a Web page they want to return to later. Bookmarking is quick and easy. But as a system for organizing information, bookmarking breaks down in at least three important ways.

If you use multiple computers, you could end up with bookmarks on one that you may need on the other. That's why I keep my bookmarks synchronized between all the computers I use, so they're always available to me, regardless of which computer I'm on.

Wish I knew what you were looking for.

—The Church, "Under the Milky Way"

For this purpose, I use Xmarks (formerly called Foxmarks), a free add-on utility for Mozilla Firefox (my browser of choice), Microsoft Internet Explorer, and Apple Safari browsers. Xmarks (www.xmarks.com) stores your bookmarks to a free online account you set up on an Xmarks server. The bookmarks you save on one computer are automatically copied to the server. When you go online with another computer, your latest bookmarks are automatically downloaded to the browser you use on that computer.

Another problem with bookmarks is that, over time, you may accumulate a lot of them, and you end up with this long, disorganized list. The reason that I use the Firefox browser is that it does the best job among browsers of letting me add tags (keywords, in essence) to my bookmarks, at the time I create them, and those tags make my bookmarks easy to search.

Let's say I come across a *Miami Herald* article online about how Trent Reznor (he of Nine Inch Nails fame) is using Twitter. I read the article, which says the band skipped its encore during a West Palm Beach concert and that Reznor quickly tweeted an explanation about what happened (a technical glitch was at fault). I'm interested in how bands use social media, so I bookmark the article. (To create a bookmark in Firefox, click "Bookmarks" in the menu bar, followed by "Bookmark This Page" in the drop-down menu. Or just use the shortcut *Control + D* in Windows or *Command + D* on a Mac.)

A Browser, an Operating System & Some Cool Stickers

A "Page Bookmarked" screen pops up, where you can change the bookmark's name—which is sometimes a good idea. By default, the bookmark's name is the same as the Web page's title. The words in the Firefox bookmark's name are searchable, so to increase your chances of finding a bookmark in a search later, you might want to rename it, to make it as descriptive as possible. In this case, the bookmark's name by default is "Nine Inch Nails' Trent Reznor is a Twitter fanatic—People—MiamiHerald.com." That's fairly descriptive, but exceptionally long, so I'll change the bookmark text to something like "Trent sends Tweet."

Then, in the same "Page Bookmarked" screen, I'll add the tags *encore, technical glitch, Twitter, West Palm Beach* (separating each tag with a comma). Now, if I want to try and remember later where it was that the Nine Inch Nails skipped an encore because of a technical glitch, and Trent Reznor tweeted about it, I can find this particular bookmark in Firefox using any combination of the words *Twitter, Trent, West Palm Beach, technical glitch, tweet,* and *encore.* (To search your bookmarks in Firefox, go to "Bookmarks" on the menu bar, select "Organize bookmarks," then type your words in the search box.)

The third challenge with bookmarks is that Web pages are sometimes ephemeral. A page you bookmarked two months ago may no longer exist when you revisit it. So if the information you find online is critical to keep (more so than Trent Reznor's Twitter activity, that is), I'd suggest you copy the Web page's content and paste it into an e-mail to yourself. You might also copy and paste into the e-mail the Web page's address in case you want to go to that specific page later, assuming it still exists. By the way, before you copy the content, it helps to click the "Format for printing" option many Web sites give you, as this usually eliminates ads and other stuff you don't want to copy. Then send the message to yourself. If you're using Gmail, you might also add a label to the message to help you find it later. Using the Nine Inch Nails example, I might add labels such as "Social Media," "Twitter," and "Nine Inch Nails" to the Gmail message I've sent myself containing that article. Then the article will present itself if I sort my messages using any of those labels, or if I just do a search in Gmail.

Engaging My Brain over the Atlantic

Of course, you won't need to store or organize the vast majority of information you read online. Most of the time, you can just skim it and move on. But even if you don't need to keep or remember that information, it helps to organize how it reaches you in the first place—so you can minimize all the jumping around you'd have to do on the Internet to get information. That's why I use Google Reader. It grabs all the latest news, blog posts, and other information I'm interested in and puts it all in one place, so I can scan it when I've got a few minutes.

Google Reader (www.google.com/reader) is a Really Simple Syndication (RSS) feed aggregator. If you know what that means, congratulations; you get to skip the next two paragraphs.

RSS is a standardized system for automatically syndicating—or "feeding"—frequently updated Web content, such as blog posts and news headlines. You subscribe to an RSS "feed," and you use an RSS feed aggregator like Google Reader to receive all those feeds in one place. You can subscribe to and read content delivered via RSS feeds in Outlook, in your browser, or in some other RSS aggregator/reader.

Feed your head.

—Jefferson Airplane,
"White Rabbit"

Let's say you're interested in books (I'm just guessing here) and you particularly enjoy the *New York Times* book coverage. Instead of having to go to the *Times* site every day to see what's new in the world of literature, you could simply subscribe to the RSS feed for the *Times*'s book coverage. Whenever the *Times* Web site publishes a new article related to books, a brief description of the article, or a sentence or two from the article itself, is automatically pushed to the RSS aggregator of your choice, such as Google Reader. To read the entire article, you click a link within the article's description sent to your RSS aggregator. The link takes you directly to the article on the *Times*'s Web site. Though many publishers use feeds to bring people like you to their sites, some—especially blogs—syndicate entire articles via RSS feeds, which means it will take you a few less steps to get to the content.

Google Reader has a really helpful Google search box, which gives you lots of ways to find your RSS items. You can search only those items you've already read; search only your starred items (you can star items just as you can star messages in Gmail); and so on.

I'm particularly happy that Google Reader works well on my iPhone, so I can catch up on what interests me while standing in a long airport security queue. Also, Google Reader makes it easy for me to share items with friends or colleagues; it's yet another way to collaborate using information of mutual interest.

As I mentioned, with Google Reader I can star any RSS item. That makes it easy to organize my items; I can filter out everything that isn't a priority for the moment, so I can focus on only what's of most importance to me. Another advantage is that Google Reader works offline, which allows me to catch up on news and blogs when I'm flying over the Atlantic without an Internet connection. There are a few steps you have to take first, however, to use Reader offline. First, you have to install Google Gears, the technology that makes using Reader and other Google products offline possible. (Alternatively, you can skip this step and just use Chrome, Google's Web browser.) Next, you have to remember to click the green "down" icon in the upper right-hand corner of your browser window when you're in Google Reader. This will tell Google Reader to download all your current RSS items to a cache on your computer's hard drive, so that Google Reader can display those items to you when you're offline.

Think About the Bread Crumbs You'll Leave

And there you have it: the most important scaffolds I use, and how and why I use them. The tricks I use to get information into my head, the tools I rely on to get stuff out of my head—and then find it later on when I need it, quickly and easily. I hope that, if nothing else, these past few chapters have given you ideas about how to organize all the bits of information that come at you every day.

Because information is so essential to being organized,

I encourage you to start thinking about building your own scaffolds, or your own system for organizing your always-expanding building of information. How do the scaffolds you're using today fail you? In what ways are they limited? What could they do better? I'm not here to tell you to do everything my way. But in my opinion, the scaffolds I've written about in these chapters are best suited for the way our brains, and the world we live in today, really work.

While you're at it, it helps to change how you think about search too, because of how important it is to organizing our information. Search shouldn't be something you do just to find stuff other people posted on the Internet. Search should be integrated into everything you do with your own information as well. When you create an e-mail reminder about something, think about the keywords you might use to find that e-mail again, whether it's one day, one week, or one decade later. When you evaluate a new scaffold, take into account how well (or badly) it lets you search for your stuff.

In other words, try to make search a forethought, not an afterthought.

A few more words of advice, if I may be so bold: Get an iPhone. Or a Google Android phone. Or any phone with a large screen, a fast Internet connection, and a Web browser experience that's as close as possible to what you'd get on a computer. Then start storing as much of your important information—documents, contacts, appointments, e-mail—in the cloud.

Do all that, and just about wherever you go, you'll have access to a huge amount of information that's important *to you*. When you need it, search for it. When someone else needs it, share it. You'll be less frantic, confused, and stressed. You'll begin to breathe a little more easily every day.

After all, search is oxygen.

ENCODE THIS

- Whenever it's practical, I create and store personal documents in the cloud with Google Docs.

- Google Docs serves my goal of collaborating

with others on basic documents particularly well. Frequently, I type meeting notes on my laptop into a Google Docs text file. I share real-time access and editing privileges for the document with the other attendees. Together, we create a richer historical record of who said what.

- Web content poses many organizational challenges. If you use multiple computers, synchronize your bookmarks between them all with a browser add-on like Xmarks. That way, the bookmarks you save on one computer are automatically copied to the other.

- Bookmarks can become really disorganized over time. Using Mozilla Firefox—which I consider to be the best browser—you can add tags to your bookmarks and you can easily search them.

- Web pages can be ephemeral. If information you find online is really important, copy and paste it into an e-mail, where it will become part of your searchable archive.

- It's equally important to organize the information you follow online. Use an RSS feed aggregator like Google Reader to automatically grab the stuff you're interested in and corral it into one place.

PRINCIPLES OF ORGANIZATION: A RECAP

1. Organize your life to minimize brain strain.

2. Get stuff out of your head as quickly as possible.

3. Multitasking can actually make you less efficient.

4. Use stories to remember.

5. Just because something's always been done a certain way doesn't mean it *should* be.

6. Knowledge is not power. The *sharing* of knowledge is power.

7. Organize around actual constraints, not assumed ones.

8. Be completely honest—but never judgmental—with yourself.

9. Know when to ignore your constraints.

10. Know exactly where you're going—and how you'll get there—before you start the engine.

11. Be flexible about the outcome of your goals.

12. Don't organize your information; search for it.

13. Only keep in your head what truly needs to be there.

14. Break big chunks into small ones.

15. Dedicate time each week to reviewing key information.

16. There's no such thing as a perfect system of organization.

17. Whenever possible, use the tools you already know.

18. Add relevant keywords to your digital information so you can easily find it later.

part three

OVERCOMING
CHALLENGES,
BIG AND
SMALL

chapter 12

AVOIDING BRAIN STRAIN

strategies for minimizing distractions
and staying focused throughout
the workday

IN THIS CHAPTER
Why It's Hard to Decide on Dinner
Strategies for Shifting Contexts
Other People: Context Shifts You Can't Always Control
Is This Meeting Really Necessary?

WHEN MY ALARM GOES off at 5:30 A.M., I pop up like a
piece of toast. An hour later, I'm in a videoconference.
The meeting—covering all sorts of administrative and strategic
stuff—goes until 10:00. My next meeting, about staffing and hir-
ing, is from 10:30 until 11:00. At 11:00, I jump into another videoconference, this one about a business deal I'm working on.

After a quick lunch break, I have two one-on-one videoconferences, each with a different direct report and on a completely different issue. From there, I meet with a major client.
Then, I have thirty minutes to answer as many e-mails as I
can squeeze in. Next, I'm off to another meeting, this one with

someone from the finance department. By the time I'm back at my desk, there are five or six unrelated tasks, all relatively time sensitive, that demand my attention—not to mention all the voicemails I have to catch up on. Before I know it, the day's over, and I'm racing out of the office and running to the grocery store to pick up the things we need for dinner.

And so goes a relatively typical day for me. I've certainly had much worse, and I'm sure you have too. But even though no particular meeting or task that day was especially difficult, the cumulative impact of them all left me mentally drained.

When you're focused on one particular type of information, challenge, or task, and then you switch to something different, you're shifting contexts. Sometimes the transitions are huge and jarring. Other times, you don't even notice them. You're e-mailing a client when a friend calls, asking for advice on a business matter. You chat with your friend, then go back to your e-mail. Without even realizing it, you've shifted contexts twice within a few minutes.

Context shifts can be beneficial. Let's say you've been churning endlessly on a work project, unable to move ahead, growing more frustrated. So you go to lunch with a colleague and talk about nothing but sports. By the time you return to the project, you've got some distance from it. Now you can see why you'd been churning, and the solution is obvious.

I run my life / Or is it running me?

—Lady Antebellum, "I Run to You"

Plus, without context shifts, you'd spend your entire day doing pretty much the same thing. That sounds extraordinarily boring, to say the least.

However, frequent context shifts can be extremely distracting and impair your ability to concentrate on the task at hand. And worse, over just the course of the day, they can seriously drain your brain's reservoir. Ever wonder why, no matter how much sleep you might have gotten the night before, you feel tired and unable to focus by 4 P.M.? It's because shifting between all the meetings, e-mails, voicemails, hallway conversations, phone calls, and tasks in your day has used up an enormous amount of brainpower, leaving you feeling depleted. And when you have no mental energy, you can't think clearly about your challenges, whether they're major or miniscule, immediate or long term, expected or unexpected. I'll explain why in a minute.

In Part Two I, I offered you tips and strategies for how to best use all the tools you have at your disposal to organize the information in your life. Well, now it's time to look at the bigger picture. In Part Three, I'll share tips and strategies for how to organize your life to better meet the challenges, big and small, that you face every day. I'll show you how to organize your day to stay more focused, and how to minimize the daily distractions and context shifts that tax your brain and leave you exhausted. We'll take a look at how to achieve a "work-life balance," or more precisely, how to *integrate* work and life. From there, it's on to the really big stuff: how to organize your life so that you're best prepared to handle— with minimal stress—a major life crisis. Let's get started.

Why It's Hard to Decide on Dinner

Let's return, for the moment, to the topic of chapter 1, about how the brain works.

As I mentioned, you need information to perform even minor tasks. With everything you do, your brain transfers information you've previously encoded from long-term to short-term memory, to help you out.

For instance, imagine you're writing an e-mail to your coworkers, recapping your impressions of an industry conference you recently attended. As you write, your brain retrieves stuff from long-term memory—what you did at the conference, whom you talked to, what you discussed, what you learned, that sort of thing. The information you encoded lives for the moment again in your short-term memory, until you finish writing the e-mail—or even before that. Then the information returns to long-term memory, where most of it will fade over time unless you call it up again later.

> Little angels of the silences / That climb into my bed and whisper.
>
> —Counting Crows, "Angels of the Silences"

Meanwhile, as you write that e-mail, new information enters your short-term memory. Maybe as you recall the conversations you had with people at the trade show, a story or a trend emerges in your mind. This aha moment is a new piece of information. It exists in your short-term memory too, until it's forgotten or transferred to long-term memory.

But remember how I said short-term memory can store between only five and nine things at once? When you shift contexts, your brain has to try to transfer whatever is currently in short-term memory—a new idea, an observation, a reminder—into long-term memory. The information has to go somewhere, to make room in your short-term memory for the information you need for the new context. It's the cognitive equivalent of an overbooked flight. The plane isn't going to take off until some passengers give up their seats.

Needless to say, just like those unfortunate passengers who get bounced, when you shift contexts, some information never makes it from short-term memory into long-term memory. It gets dropped as the new information floods in.

And so it goes, all day, every day. The more you shift contexts, and the more unrelated those contexts are, the harder your brain works to transfer, store, and flush information out of short-term memory to make room for more. And it doesn't just drop the things you no longer need; it drops things that are crucial to your ability to function. You may have to decide on your goals for each new context too. Why are you writing that e-mail to your colleagues? Who are these people you're about to have a meeting with, and what do they want from you? What are your objectives for the meeting?

The telephone is ringing / You got me on the run.

—Alice Cooper, "Under My Wheels"

Adjusting your brain to new contexts is difficult to do. Multiply the effort involved in each context shift by the dozen that you make over the course of a long day, and it's no wonder you struggle just deciding what to eat for dinner.

Lots of context switching during a day also adds stress. If you're trying to focus on accomplishing a specific task, and you keep getting distracted, you'll get frustrated. Once you reach frustration, it's just a short stroll to Stressville. The more stressed you become, the harder it can be to focus. Suddenly, you're reunited with your old friend, the downward spiral.

Strategies for Shifting Contexts

Often, you have zero control over context shifts. You're working intently on a marketing plan when your boss calls you into an urgent, mandatory budget meeting. What are you supposed to do? Say "Thanks, but I can't afford an abrupt context shift right now"?

But now, the good news. There are ways you can reduce the number of context shifts you make every day. And, more importantly, you can minimize their side effects and lessen the toll each one takes on your brain.

Here's a trick to get you started (it's also my organization principle no. 20): *Take notes to help you shift contexts later.* As I mentioned in chapter 10, I always try to add background information to a new calendar entry. If it's a business meeting, my assistant or I will add notes to the appointment entry about whom I'm meeting with, what the meeting's goals are, the location's address and driving directions to it (if it's off-site), and so on. That way, I've got some background information to help me transition into the business meeting's context. I don't have to waste my time or anyone else's trying to recall basic stuff from long-term memory, like what the meeting is about. The information I need to transition into the meeting without feeling disoriented is right in front of me. And it's searchable too, so I can find it again later, if needed.

> Take notes to help you shift contexts later.

It's also a good idea to structure your day, whenever possible, so that tasks or meetings with similar contexts—whether those meetings and tasks are on the same topic, related to the same project, or simply use the same part of your brain—fall consecutively after one another. For example, if I know that in a given week, I'll have to hold three meetings about our quarterly performance, I'll try to schedule them back-to-back so I don't have to shift in and out of the budget context. (See the sidebar "Is This Meeting Really Necessary?" for thoughts about making meetings more productive.)

Or let's say I have to attend a presentation that relates to a project I'm working on. I'll try to set aside time after the presentation to work on some task related to that project. I find that when I can do that, I'm much more productive and focused because *my brain is already in that context.* When I can go from one context to a similar one, it's easier on my brain because I don't have to flush so much out of my short-term memory, and I don't have to try to remember what my goals are for the new context. I can dive right into the new task, with little mental effort. It's kind of like the way the body works in physical exercise: Since my brain has already been warmed up, I can launch right into my workout. The less I have to do those things, the less mentally exhausted I am by nightfall. This is the idea behind organization principle no. 21: *Group tasks with similar contexts together.* When planning your day, give some thought to the various contexts you'll be moving in and out of, and try to group similar ones together. Pay attention to which contexts may be more demanding than others too. If possible, save the easier ones— for example, returning phone calls from people seeking information you already know—for when you're most likely to be mentally tired.

> **Group tasks with similar contexts together.**

In chapter 3, I talked about recognizing your individual constraints—the ways in which you get in your own way. In this spirit of self-honesty, I'd encourage you to think now about the *voluntary* context shifts you make every day. Maybe you're frequently popping out of PowerPoint and into eBay. What's up with that? Are you overwhelmed, intimidated, or just bored by the presentation you're working on? Maybe something bigger is at work here. Have you always been easily distracted? Could you be a closet procrastinator? Whatever the reason, try to identify it and organize around it.

Let's say you're the easily distracted type, and e-mail—probably the most universally distracting thing in our world today—is a particular challenge for you. Whenever there's a chime on your computer alerting you to an incoming e-mail, you can't help but stop what you're doing and read the message. Not only that, you have an uncontrollable urge to reply to the e-mail *right away*, even though it's not urgent. And then another, and another, and then—wait, what was it you were doing before you replied to that e-mail?

> Wait until the dust settles / You live, you learn.
> —Alanis Morissette, "You Learn"

If that sounds like you, maybe it's time to change your e-mail software's settings so your computer doesn't chime when new messages arrive. Or set it up so you have to manually hit the Send/Receive button to check for new messages. Then, when taking a much-needed break from doing something hard, you can retrieve messages that have accumulated since you last checked. Lots of books on organization recommend designating a few set times for checking and replying to e-mail. There's a good reason to do that: because shifting between your work project and your e-mail contexts only a few times a day, instead of dozens, makes you more efficient and more focused, and it minimizes the strain on your brain.

E-mail is just one example of digital tools that can distract you. I also get text messages, I send (and follow) Twitter tweets, and I love YouTube. All of these are great for getting your mind off the hard stuff you're doing. But they can also be disruptive, if you aren't disciplined. Try to restrict your digital distractions to breaks you take between chunks of work. Despite what some people think, taking breaks (within reason) can actually make you more productive, not less. Resting your brain in between challenging tasks helps you recharge your mental energy and embark on the new task more refreshed. The trick is to think of breaks as rewards for work accomplished, rather than as ways to avoid work.

Other People: Context Shifts You Can't Always Control

Other People: Context Shifts You Can't Always Control

Then there are the many *involuntary* context shifts you face every day—namely, other people. You're particularly vulnerable to those shifts if you work in a cubicle. In that environment, anyone who happens by can throw you into a new context. (I doubt that's his or her goal, but that's the effect.)

This isn't always a bad thing. In fact, the reason your company puts practically everyone in cubicles is to foster employee collaboration (and yes, to save money). But there are times when you're on deadline. You need all your brainpower, and you don't have time for frequent interruptions. How do you prevent those distractions when you work in a cubicle?

You might rearrange your workspace so that you sit with your back to your cube's entrance. That way, you won't be as easily distracted by someone who walks by, and that person won't be able to easily get your attention. But don't stop there. You might also hang a DO NOT DISTURB—ON DEADLINE sign, or something to that effect. Put it in plain sight at your cube's entrance. Pop in some earplugs too, or listen to music on your iPod (if you're one of those people who can concentrate while listening to music, that is). Do whatever it takes to drown out the ambient noise around you. Turn off your cell phone and office phone ringers. Move your phones so their caller ID screens are out of sight, so you won't see who's calling and start wondering *why* he or she is calling, and then be tempted to answer.

Even if you have an office, you'll probably bump into coworkers when you head to the kitchen for another cup of coffee. Suddenly, a colleague wants to talk about something completely unrelated to what you've been working on at your desk. This can be a good context shift, however. Water-cooler chat can lead to new ideas and innovations, or at least to a stronger camaraderie. Plus, if you're on a coffee break, it probably means your brain needed a rest from what it was doing anyway.

Probably the most important thing you can do every day is to dedicate some time for yourself, even if it's just ten to

Meetings *are* necessary in the business world, though they're not exactly popular. The best ones are productive. The worst ones make you feel like you've been pulled away from actually getting work done, just to sit around and listen to people blather on about nothing.

A lot of companies have gone to great lengths to try to make meetings more productive. Some have banned laptops, BlackBerrys, and other devices entirely in an effort to get everyone to focus. And there's even a process called Scrum,[1] in which meetings are typically kept to fifteen minutes and all attendees are required to stay on their feet. As you can imagine, this helps make sure the meetings are brief and focused.

This is all fine and good, but to them, and to you, I ask a simple question: Wouldn't it make more sense to challenge whether a meeting is truly necessary in the first place?

When you call a meeting, be absolutely clear about its goals. Ask yourself if those goals could be just as easily accomplished some other way, such as through e-mail or phone calls. (Be careful not to overly rely on e-mail and phone conversations, however. People need occasional face time together to brainstorm and develop camaraderie.) And make sure everyone you've asked to attend the meeting really needs to be there. There's nothing more frustrating, or unproductive, than having to waste hours of your day in a meeting that has absolutely no relevance to what you do.

If a meeting truly is required, try to make everyone's shift into that context easier. For example, distribute in advance any materials you'll be discussing. This helps everyone be better informed *before* going into the meeting and helps them shift into the meeting context with less strain on their brains. Plus, everyone saves time, and the discussion is more likely to be productive.

I try to limit meetings to thirty minutes or less. It helps me, and everyone else, stay focused when we know we only

(*cont.*)

have half an hour. Besides, people tend to lose interest when meetings go on for too long. If we need more time, we're all feeling inspired and productive, and we aren't about to get kicked out of the conference room, we can keep going after thirty minutes. It makes more sense to stay in the context, as long as the energy is still there, than it does to slavishly quit at thirty minutes, only to have to reconvene—that is, shift contexts again—later. Keeping meetings to thirty minutes or less is the ideal, but it's not always practical.

If you have a meeting in which some attendees participate remotely, share meeting notes in real time with them, as I described in chapter 11. This won't necessarily reduce distractions. But it will help remote participants understand what's being said, and who's speaking.

Videoconferences can be more effective than conference calls, provided that you've got a fast Internet connection and good equipment. At least in a videoconference, you can see how others react. That can give you helpful information you'd never get in a conference call. You can conduct one-on-one video chats in Gmail, Skype (skype.com), and other messaging services. You can have multiparty video chats using Apple's iChat software (which comes preinstalled free on Macs). A number of affordable services, such as SightSpeed Business (sightspeed.com/business) and ooVoo (oovoo.com), also allow multiple parties to video chat together.

fifteen minutes. Block that time out on your work calendar (especially if others in the company have access to your calendar), so no one can claim it. Use the time to clear your mind, calm your senses, organize your tasks, or to think beyond what's happening in the moment. Think about where you are in your goals now, where you want to be later, and what's standing in your way. Look at the forest, not the trees. Give some thought to who can help you achieve your goals, and how you might collaborate with them. And as always, take notes. You'll want them later.

When you regularly give yourself time to "just think," and when you guard that time, you'll be better prepared for the ultimate context shift—the transition from the here and now to the future.

Oh yes, I almost forgot: Get a good night's sleep too. Shifting contexts is a lot easier when both you *and* your brain are rested.

ENCODE THIS

- When you're in one particular environment, or you're focusing on a particular challenge or set of information, and then you do something unrelated, you're shifting contexts.

- When you shift contexts, your brain has to transfer whatever is currently in short-term memory into long-term memory to make room for new information. Some information gets dropped along the way.

- The more you shift contexts, and the more unrelated those contexts are, the harder your brain has to work.

- You can't eliminate context shifts, but you can reduce their impact. Examples:

  - Leave notes for yourself that you can consult when shifting contexts later, to make the transition easier.

  - Group tasks or meetings with similar contexts together.

  - Identify what distractions cause you to make unnecessary, frequent context shifts, so you can reduce them.

  - Check e-mail only during breaks, instead of having it constantly interrupting your concentration.

○ Turn your phone off when you need to focus. Hide your phone's caller ID screen too, so you won't be curious about who's calling and why—which is itself a context shift.

○ If you work in a cube, hang up a DO NOT DISTURB sign when you're under deadline pressure. Wear earplugs to block ambient noise. Sit with your back to your cube's entrance, so you won't be distracted by the people walking by.

○ Carve out time every workday for yourself, even if it's just ten to fifteen minutes. Block that time out on your shared work calendar, so no one can nab it.

○ Question the need for each meeting proposed. Make sure meetings have clearly defined goals and that everyone understands them. Distribute in advance background information to help others shift contexts.

chapter 13

CHECKING E-MAIL FROM THE BEACH

how to integrate work and life

REMEMBER HOW, IN THE previous chapter, I said a good night's sleep is so important? Well, here I am, drafting this chapter at 9:30 P.M. in London. And though I'm normally ready to crash by 10:00 P.M. or so on weeknights, my body and mind are wide awake. They think it's only 1:30 in the afternoon because in California, where I've just traveled from, it *is* 1:30 in the afternoon. My mind and body don't care that I've been working since 7:00 A.M. London time, which they think was 11:00 P.M. the night before. They'd go to a rock con-cert right now, if I let them. But, alas, I have work to do.

> I hurt myself today / To see if I still feel.
>
> —Nine Inch Nails, "Hurt"

Did someone just mention a "work-life balance"? What is that, exactly, and why is it so elusive?

The "work-life balance" is the ultimate goal many people have when they strive to be better organized, or to have a more fulfilling life. It makes sense. The more efficient you are at work, the more time you have to spend on, well, life. The idea behind "work-life balance" is not to let your work life overtake your personal life, like ivy crawling up a brick wall. You work hard, yes. But you also work hard to maintain boundaries between work and everything else.

A nice idea, isn't it? And yet, fearless readers, have you noticed that a "work-life balance" seems beyond your grasp? These days, our employers expect us to do more, and usually, to do it with fewer resources. In boom times, we work long hours to try to keep up with all the business opportunities. When the economy dips, we work long hours because we want to keep our jobs and because we're also doing the work once done by colleagues who were laid off. With e-mail, BlackBerrys, videoconferencing, fast Internet access at home, cheap communication costs, and other technological advances, it's harder than ever to stop working.

Then there's the disconnect between our nine-to-five tradition and the way we really need to work. The nine-to-five constraint is particularly challenging if you have to deal with people in other time zones or if you must travel great distances in your work. How can someone living in California hope to contain work to a nine-to-five schedule if 9 A.M. for them falls toward the end of the workday for their European colleagues? The time difference alone pretty much ensures that work happens beyond the boundaries of the traditional workday on all sides of the globe.

By now, you're probably wondering why I keep putting quotation marks around "work-life balance."

I use the quotation marks because I believe that if "work-life balance" were a song, I'd file it somewhere between Sheryl Crow's "The Difficult Kind" and the show tune "The Impossible Dream." In other words, I don't believe it actually exists. Certainly the *desire* for a "work-life balance" is real. Anyone who's toiled in a high-stress job has felt a desperate need to regain personal time from work time—kind of like the Dutch reclaiming land from the sea. Families in which both parents work long hours are particularly affected by the loss of time together.

So how do we achieve a "work-life balance"? To put it succinctly, we don't, because in today's white-collar world, a "work-life balance" is a mirage.

If you listen closely, you'll notice that when most people talk about a "work-life balance," what they're really saying is they want to "work less." Fair enough; I can identify with that.

But, sorry, I'm not going to give you a chapter you can thrust into your boss's hands while you say, "See, the Google guy says I should be working less!"

A more realistic goal is to *integrate* your work with your life in a way that reduces your stress, rids you of resentments, boosts your productivity, and puts you more in sync with the joys and challenges of your life. That's what my organization principle no. 22 is all about: *Integrate work with life instead of trying to balance the two.*

> Take this job and shove it / I ain't working here no more.
>
> —Dead Kennedys, "Take This Job and Shove It"

> **Integrate work with life instead of trying to balance the two.**

Thinking Differently

To integrate work with life requires thinking differently about them both.

For starters, it helps to realize that work and life are not two separate things. Instead, I've accepted the fact that much of my life revolves around what I do for a living, just as I bring much of who I am in my personal life to my work. And that's okay. I've also accepted that sometimes I have to work a lot, and at other times, I get to play a lot. Ideally, I do some of both every day. I know that work never really stops for me, just as I know that life happens during workdays. I've given up trying to force each one into its own compartment. All that did was make me cranky and tired.

There are lots of ways to integrate work with life. Let's start with the small stuff.

In chapter 10, I talked about the advantages of organizing your calendars not by differentiating work and personal appointments but by who needs access to them. That's one small but important step toward integrating work and life. For example, you might have a Google calendar specifically for business travel and evening work engagements. And you share that calendar with your family, so they'll know when they'll see you and when they won't.

Now let's take a look at the typical workday. Generally, you're probably expected in the office most weekdays from 9:00 to 5:00, give or take a few hours, right? But aren't there times when things slow down a bit during your workday? Days when you don't *really* need to be there at 9:00 or stay until 5:00? That's true for me, even with my hectic schedule. Sometimes, I've gone home around 1:30, during a lull at work. I'll hang out with Sonya and our dogs or do something that relaxes me. Then I'll go back to the office and work for several more hours.

> The spaceman says, "Everybody look down / It's all in your mind."
> —The Killers, "Spaceman"

If you've got a long commute to work, however, going home for a siesta is probably not an option. But is there a gym nearby? A park? A movie theater you can sneak off to? Someplace you can go and shut your brain off for a little while? Whatever you do, taking time out when work is slow helps you relax and clear your mind.

This is key. Part of why you're stressed is because you're not just working 9 to 5; you're doing stuff, like answering work e-mail, beyond those hours. However, by snatching time for yourself during the day when work's slower, and by working when there's work to do—even if it's 10 P.M. —you're just adjusting your habits according to what your workday *actually* looks like, rather than trying to organize your life around the way you *think* it should be.

There's another benefit to this strategy. Sometimes, I resent the fact that I'm constantly receiving work-related e-mail, and that I always seem to be behind. But if I take time for myself during the workday when there's a lull, I can answer work e-mail late at night and not feel as if I'm giving up something. It feels like a quid pro quo, instead of an intrusion or a sacrifice.

Then there's the question of working on weekends. If my choice is between door no. 1, where I take care of work-related voicemail and e-mail here and there on Saturdays and Sundays, or door no. 2, in which I face an onslaught of urgent messages first thing Monday mornings, I'll gladly take door no. 1, thank you. When I attend to work-related messages on weekends, though, I tend to do it from my iPhone while doing something boring, like standing in a supermarket checkout line. This way, I don't feel like I'm giving up anything fun or worthwhile (except the chance to scan tabloid headlines), and I feel like I'm making good use of the otherwise wasted downtime.

Another important strategy in integrating work and life is something I referred to a few paragraphs back: working smarter.

If you don't organize your work well, if you procrastinate often, if you waste lots of time checking sports scores or reading the news online at your desk, you're prolonging your workday—without really giving your brain a break. Breaks are restorative only if they truly are breaks, which means that you're away from your desk and your computer and doing something that gives your brain a rest. This will help you stay focused, organized, and on task when it's time to work, which in turn makes you more efficient and gives you more quality time later to be with friends or family, or to enjoy some quality time with yourself.

If all this sounds easy, trust me: It's not.

There's a reason the BlackBerry is called the "CrackBerry." Because it's so easy to stay connected to work at just about any moment, that's exactly what we do. It's a drug all right, only more dangerous because often we don't even know we're addicted.

I see this manifested in many ways. Often, when I'm in a restaurant with Sonya, I look around at the nearby tables. Inevitably, I'll notice several people "subtly" checking e-mail on their phones. I hate to tell you, dude, but this isn't a "work-life balance." This is pretending your life, and the people in it, don't exist.

So what's the difference between checking e-mail when you're having dinner with your beloved versus when you're standing in the supermarket checkout line? In the first scenario, you're willingly losing a moment that should be devoted to a pleasurable life experience. Not to mention that it's just plain rude.

In the second situation, however, you're not giving up anything, unless you love standing in checkout lines. Instead, you're being productive during what's usually a tedious, thankless task. In my opinion, that counts as a gain, not a loss. In fact, I maintain a list (in Things, my to-do application) of "five-minute tasks." These are little things I need to get done but aren't difficult or aren't especially connected to other things I'm doing. And, as you might expect, given the name, they usually take about five minutes. For example, one task might be to make a dinner reservation for Valentine's Day at a favorite restaurant. Another might be to respond to an e-mail from someone at work, or to call my friend about helping me set up a home media server. Usually, I can check all of these off my list fairly easily while standing in the grocery store (or drugstore or car wash or dry cleaner) line. This is what I mean by work-life integration.

Check E-mail on Vacation?

Vacations can be a particularly challenging time if you're still trying to balance work and life, rather than integrate them.

Should you check e-mail and voicemail on a much-needed holiday? Do you take that urgent phone call or let it go to voicemail? Or do you leave your work cell phone at home and only take your personal phone? Maybe you don't take a phone with you at all?

I can't offer a one-size-fits-all rule here. The fact is, some of us need an extended break from even thinking about work. How will you truly feel like an inhabitant of that charming Tuscan village you're visiting when you're frequently answering e-mails from coworkers back home? Yet others worry so much about the e-mail and voicemail messages piling up during their absence, they get squirrelly if they don't attend to them on vacation. And they spend the entire vacation dreading the prospect of weeding through them all when the vacation's over.

I fall into the latter category. I'd rather take care of business, at least a little bit each day, on vacation. Otherwise, I worry that I'll turn on my computer when I get back to work and it will be like that scene from the Marx Brothers movie *A Night at the Opera*, where someone opens a cruise ship cabin door and about twenty people come tumbling out.

But that's just me. If you're the type that needs a complete rest from your routine once or twice a year, that's cool. Go on that bungee jumping trip to New Zealand and leave the CrackBerry at home. Just be sure to set expectations with others. Set up an automated e-mail reply that informs people you're unavailable, when you'll be back, and whom to contact in your absence. (Gmail and most other e-mail systems let you create automated e-mail replies that go only to people in your address book, so you won't inadvertently confirm your e-mail address to spammers.) On the other hand, if you're the type to worry so much about what's going on back at the office that you can't relax or enjoy yourself (which, after all, is the whole point of taking a vacation in the first place), you might check messages once a day, in the morning. After that, you can forget about work and enjoy the rest of the day with a clear conscience. Whichever you choose to do, have a plan before you leave for vacation and try to stick to it.

Frequent Frying

Frequent international business travel is one of the biggest work-life challenges I face on a regular basis. I spend countless hours in airports, in taxis on the way to and from airports, in the air, in hotels, and in different time zones. The long trips eat up enormous amounts of time and leave me feeling fried.

I could grumble and complain about it (and I do). But that doesn't make the situation any better. So I try to make the

most of all the dead time on these long international trips.
While in flight, I will usually work for several hours. I wrote a
lot of this book somewhere over the Atlantic, in fact, so that
when I was back home, I could spend more time with Sonya
and the dogs and less time writing.

I travel with an Amazon Kindle e-book reader too, so on the
plane or while I'm waiting in line at the airport, I can catch up
on whatever book I'm reading. I usually load lots of e-books
on my Kindle (it beats lugging them in my carry-on), so if I
finish one during my trip, I can start another—or I can buy a
new e-book from the Kindle online store in just a few minutes.
(The Kindle uses a cellular wireless network to connect you
to the Amazon Kindle store.) I can also buy and download to
my Kindle that day's edition of the *New York Times* (or other
newspapers and magazines). Plus, since I also receive many
of my work-related documents as PDF files, or save them in
that format, I can e-mail those documents to my Kindle. And
suddenly, that performance review I have to read appears in
my Kindle queue just above my favorite sci-fi novel. *Voilá!*—
another integration of work and life. I always bring or buy a
few magazines with me too, for those times during the flight
when you can't use electronic devices.

As I mentioned in chapter 11, during long flights I also
catch up on news, blogs, and other information using Google
Reader in offline mode. But I find I can use this downtime
productively even without my gadgets. I try to spend some of
the travel time thinking about problems I'm facing at work,
or making plans for the future. For that, I carry one of my
Moleskine notebooks or a regular notepad, so I can get my
ideas down on paper.

I also try to take good care of myself on these trips; nothing drains my productivity more than fatigue and jet lag. For
example, when I'm traveling internationally, I always try to
arrive in the middle of the afternoon, so I'll have time to eat
and relax my mind before the local clock tells me it's bed-
time. I try to sleep a lot that first night because I know I need
the extra rest. And each morning, I exercise in my hotel room
for at least a few minutes because exercise is important to

me. It makes me feel good, it's great for lessening stress, and it relaxes my brain.

Speaking of my brain, jet lag really does a number on it. When we're jetlagged, we tend to be more forgetful and have much more trouble staying focused for long periods of time. That's because the process of shifting contexts from one place and time zone to another, compounded by the loss of sleep, depletes us of excess brain power.

But there are ways around this, using some of the tools and systems I've developed for organizing. For example, on international business trips, during which I know I'm more prone to lapses in memory, I do several things to minimize the amount of stuff I try to keep in my short-term memory.

For one, I enter all new tasks I think of into my to-do application, Things, on my iPhone, even if they're seemingly obvious ones such as "Ask hotel for wake-up call." Anytime something comes to me that I might need to do or follow up on when I get home, I write that down immediately too. I don't sort or prioritize any of the to-dos; I just want to get them out of my head. Then, once I've returned, I sort through the tasks I've entered. Often, to-dos that seemed important while I was away don't seem worth doing once I'm home. That's okay. At least I didn't forget something important because my brain was overstressed.

Not to get all gushy on you, but you want to know the worst part about frequent, international business travel? I miss my wife and our dogs, our home, my favorite orange juice…you get the picture. And they miss me. Well, the house and orange juice don't, but I can live with that. Luckily, though, thanks to all the amazing communication tools we have today, it's much easier to stay connected to people while traveling on business. Video chats aren't the same as being there, of course, but being able to see your loved ones as well as talk to them does takes some of the sting out of being far away from home.

When I was at EMI, it was seriously challenging to stay connected, given the eight-hour time difference between London and Los Angeles. When Sonya was getting up, I was in afternoon meetings. When she was having a nice lunch in the sunshine, I was wrapping up a dinner meeting. As I was preparing for bed, it was the middle of her afternoon.

So we devised a plan. The first thing I'd do when I woke up in London was check my personal e-mail. Sonya always sent me a good-night e-mail before she went to bed, telling me about her day. It was as if she were telling me good-night—or was it good morning?—in person. I'd respond with an e-mail telling her how I slept, and I'd reply to stuff she mentioned in her e-mail. During the day, we'd send each other a few text messages; that was about all we had time for during our heavily scheduled workdays. When I was going to bed, I sent Sonya my version of the good-night e-mail.

> **The sun is settin' like molasses in the sky.**
>
> —Alannah Myles, "Black Velvet"

Through this ritual, we stayed as close as possible despite the distance between us. My brain and my body were in another time zone. But I knew all about the goofy-looking boots Sonya saw someone wearing, or the interesting conversation she had with a friend, or what had been going on with the dogs. And with those little bits of information in my head, I could begin, at last, to drift off to sleep.

ENCODE THIS

- The "work-life balance" is the ultimate goal many people have in mind when they think about getting organized. Given the world we live in today, however, it's usually an unrealistic goal.

- When most people talk about a "work-life balance," what they're really saying is they want to "work less." But in today's highly competitive, always-connected world, this really isn't possible. A more realistic goal is to *integrate* your work with your life in a way that reduces your stress, boosts your productivity, and puts you more in sync with the joys and challenges of your life.

- To integrate work with life requires you to think

differently about them both. First, stop seeing them as two separate things that fit neatly into individual compartments. Accept the fact that sometimes we have to work a lot, and at other times, we get to play a lot. Work doesn't have to stop to make room for life, just as life doesn't have to take a backseat to work.

- You can start integrating work with life with your calendar. Set up calendars based on who needs access to them, not on artificial boundaries between work and life.

- Take time out during the workday for yourself, when work is slower. It will help you relax and clear your mind. Then you won't feel like you're giving up too much if you take care of business after hours. And you won't have worked harder, necessarily. You'll have worked smarter because you gave your brain a chance to rest and recharge.

- If you take care of work in microbits throughout the weekend, during dead time or while doing routine or mindless tasks, you'll be less likely to feel resentful. And you'll turn tedious tasks into productive work time.

- If you don't organize your workday well, you're just prolonging it, without giving your brain a rest. Staying focused, organized, and on task when it's time to work gives you more quality time to enjoy with friends or family, or even just yourself.

- Should you check messages on vacation, or make the world go away? The answer depends on your goals for the vacation, your needs, and your constraints. Whatever the answer, come up with a plan before you leave.

- Frequent international business travel is one of the biggest work-life challenges. It's important to take care of yourself however possible: Get a little exercise in your hotel room, get to bed early, and stay connected with your loved ones. Filter like crazy; your brain doesn't need to be taxed any more than necessary. And because you'll have less excess mental capacity, get stuff out of your head right away. Capture to-dos and reminders on your phone or in a notebook—whatever's handy.

DEALING WITH
THE UNEXPECTED

I'M CRUISING ON MY motorcycle, the sun's on my face, life is good. Suddenly, the driver of a black SUV swerves into my lane.

To avoid a collision, I hit my brakes so hard they squeal. My front tire is smoking. I nearly lose my balance—if not my life. My heart's pounding, my life passes before my eyes, I can taste the adrenaline. I pull over to the side of the road, breathe, and try to calm myself. I can't continue, at least not yet.

Whether you ride motorcycles or not, you've probably faced something sudden, unexpected, and scary too. It may have been in your face, like the situation I just described. But sometimes, a tectonic shift happens right under your feet, and you might not even realize it, not in that moment. The shift begins in slow motion and then picks up velocity. There's no way you could have planned for it. And when the earth finally stops moving, you wonder what happened. You've lost your confidence, you're not sure how you'll get through it. Why aren't you able to cope better? Why have your organizational skills failed you?

When you're faced with huge, unexpected challenges, everything in your world gets tested. Remember how I said we're bad at making decisions? During times of high anxiety, it's more difficult than ever to make reasonable, unemotional decisions. You can't concentrate. You forget things because you're stressed, you're stressed because you forget things, and there you go, down that spiral again. In AA language, you hit bottom.

> **I'm flirtin' with disaster every day.**
>
> —Molly Hatchet, "Flirtin' with Disaster"

The biggest challenges we face in life—an economic meltdown, an illness, the death of a loved one—stem from events we can't control. I can't keep the driver in front of me from making a sudden lane change any more than you can avoid big, unexpected challenges in your life. Is it possible, though, to get through an unexpected ordeal with as little stress as possible?

Yes. Easy, it's not. But the key is to spend time getting organized *before* a crisis strikes, which in turn helps you prepare for the unexpected when it comes. Think of your organizational skills as insurance against that head-on collision.

I learned this lesson from the overwhelming challenges I faced during an extraordinarily trying and difficult time in my life.

An Unfortunate Series of Misunderstandings

The story began one morning in February 2006. Jeanne and I had been living together for several years, in the San Francisco Bay Area. I was working for Google in Mountain View; she'd just started a new position at a pharmaceutical company in San Diego.

We had decided to sell our house in the Bay Area. The plan was for me to get an apartment near Google headquarters in Mountain View. Jeanne and I would buy a house in San Diego, and I'd fly down on weekends.

On one particular morning, I was preparing to leave on a

business trip when I noticed Jeanne's blue eyes had a slight yellowish tint. And she'd developed a rash on her lower back. Both seemed a little odd, but neither of us thought too much of them. Jeanne agreed to call her general practitioner in San Diego. Then we went our separate ways, as planned: I flew off on my business trip, Jeanne headed to San Diego.

Jeanne managed to get an appointment with her doctor for the next day. After examining her, he suspected she had hepatitis and ordered some blood tests. Twenty-four hours later, after the test results came back, Jeanne's doctor told her it appeared she had an autoimmune disorder that was destroying her liver.

The doctor recommended a liver transplant. Even then, the average life expectancy was about ten years.

Jeanne was scared and upset. I felt completely powerless. I knew I had to do something, anything. I researched liver transplants online. I got tested to see if I could be a donor for her (no dice). I talked to everyone I knew, in hopes of finding a compatible donor. I tried to learn as much as possible about liver donations and transplants. All the while, I was trying to cheer Jeanne up.

A few days passed. I was still on my business trip, in an airport somewhere in the Midwest, waiting to catch a flight to Phoenix. Jeanne called to tell me she was going to see a liver specialist in San Diego, to verify her diagnosis. A friend was going to drive her. I told Jeanne I loved her, and that I'd talk to her later.

That night, I called Jeanne's cell phone, but got her voicemail. I assumed she was sleeping, so I texted her, asking her to call me. By the next morning, she hadn't responded to either my text or my voicemail. I didn't know what was going on. Was she angry with me? Was she okay? Was the news that bad? I called every few hours, almost stalker-like. Each time, I got the same response: voicemail, voicemail, voicemail.

A couple more days came and went. I was in Phoenix, trying to focus on work but feeling increasingly frantic, barely holding myself together. I called a close friend from Los Angeles and told him what was happening. Without hesitation, he said he'd meet me in San Diego and suggested I get there as soon as possible. On the way to the airport, I wondered what we would do when we arrived in San Diego. I didn't have a phone number for Jeanne's friend. In fact, I didn't even know the friend's last name. I didn't know the name of the liver specialist Jeanne had seen.

As I thought about this, a terrible image crossed my mind. I began to worry that, instead of being angry at me, Jeanne had died and that, for whatever reason, no one was able to reach me.

As I was waiting to board my flight, my cell phone rang. It was Jeanne. *"Why haven't you called me?"* I asked, my voice harsh with fear-turned-anger.

A pause. When Jeanne spoke, it was in a thin, weak voice; her breathing sounded labored.

When she went in for her tests at the hospital, Jeanne slowly explained, she gave her friend her clothes, laptop, and cell phone to hang on to. The hospital staff gave Jeanne the ultrasound and discovered her liver was healthy.

They also discovered an eight-centimeter mass blocking the duct to her gall bladder.

Jeanne had undergone an emergency surgery to get a biopsy of the mass and to clear the duct so that bile could pass out of her liver. The surgery took several hours. She hadn't called, Jeanne explained, because her friend had her cell phone. The friend didn't turn on the phone while Jeanne was in the hospital. Sedated for the surgery, Jeanne wasn't coherent enough to tell her friend she wanted to talk to me, and the friend didn't understand this was what Jeanne wanted. And so, through an unfortunate series of misunderstandings (among other things), Jeanne and I spent three terrifying days unable to reach each other.

At the time, Jeanne and I didn't have a plan for communicating. We didn't know we needed one until then, by which time everything was happening quickly. In hindsight, I should have made a point of getting Jeanne's friend's full name and cell phone number, as well as the name of the doctor she was going to see. Given that we lived in California, a state not unfamiliar with natural disasters, we should have had a plan for emergency communications too.

Fighting the Battle, and Winning

The surgery was just the beginning. Jeanne's official diagnosis was cholangiocarcinoma—a $25 word meaning bile duct cancer. For those of you playing the game at home, this is not a diagnosis you want to receive.

Jeanne started chemotherapy right away. She spent hours at the Infusion Center at the Stanford Cancer Center, watching movies or listening to music (probably Elton John) on her computer. She was making the best of it.

By May, she had outlived her initial prognosis. She was twenty pounds lighter, her once pearl-white skin was mottled and yellow, and though her eyes were still bright blue, she wasn't quite able to smile.

She was beautiful.

But we had reached a milestone. The chemotherapy wasn't working. Her cancer was terminal. All we could do was wait, love each other, and try to manage her fear and pain. We arranged for hospice care and a full-time home nurse. Jeanne's mother came to stay with us, to care for her as well.

On June 23, Jeanne asked me not to go to work. Around 1:30 P.M., she was in bed, slipping in and out of consciousness. I was holding her hand, telling her I loved her, that it was time to let go, and that we'd all be fine.

A few minutes later, Jeanne looked at me and managed a smile. It was faint, but it reminded me of the first of her smiles I ever saw. My eyes filled with tears and a sob broke from my throat.

"Okay," she said. "I'm ready." I told her good-bye and thanked her for being in my life.

> Angels with silver wings /
> Shouldn't know suffering.
>
> —Depeche Mode, "Precious"

At 1:40 P.M., Jeanne Michele Russell died. She'd fought a battle with cancer and won.

A Little Help from My Friends

It's amazing how many things I didn't understand during Jeanne's illness. At times, I'm still angry with myself about how many things I got wrong. And I'm angry I'll never have another chance to get it right, at least not with Jeanne.

One example: Toward the end, Jeanne slept in a bedroom down the hall. Her mother would sleep in a chair near her all night. So I slept in my bedroom down the hall. Later, Sonya asked why I hadn't set up another bed in Jeanne's room, so I could be with her during the night.

Why? Because I hadn't thought of it. The point is, I could go on beating myself up about this forever, or I could recognize that because I was weak, tired, and stressed, my brain and my reasoning were impaired. This is something I still struggle with and probably will for some time. But the experience has at least taught me this lesson: In stressful times, we're never really prepared for the decisions we'll have to make or the challenges we'll have to face. The best we can do is to minimize all the other, relatively unimportant stresses in our lives, so we can focus our mental energy on the things that really matter. And we have to accept the fact we're going to make mistakes during stressful times. The mistakes will probably feel even bigger than they would under ordinary circumstances. But we must try to accept this as part of the process, to not beat ourselves up over it.

> I've been swimming in a sea of anarchy.
>
> —Sheryl Crow, "Every Day is a Winding Road"

Too Much Information

When you're facing a huge challenge, a typical response is to seek more information. Information helps us feel in control, capable of dealing with the problem at hand. Unfortunately, it's easy to feel overwhelmed by all the information we're receiving, especially if it's conflicting or outside our areas of knowledge. As I mentioned earlier, managing Jeanne's illness involved dealing with enormous amounts of information, which posed a great number of organizational challenges. But organizational systems are like car insurance: Having them in place won't prevent the crash or even reduce the damage, but it will help you deal with the accident with the least amount of stress and hassle.

Given all the different physicians and kinds of treatment Jeanne received, it was hugely difficult to just keep the appointments straight, not to mention all the organizational challenges of making sure she was scheduled for the right treatments, had transportation to get there, and so forth. And each time there was a change in the routine, it had to be communicated to various caregivers.

For each change in medication, we wrote up a new set of instructions. But even then, it was difficult. Many medication names are long, seemingly random strings of characters, and some medications have similar names. Which one did the doctor mean for us to change? How many times a day is she supposed to take this one? When is she supposed to stop taking that one?

To help us get through this, we started tape-recording most doctor appointments and taking pages of notes. I tried to store copies of our notes everywhere, both in paper form in Jeanne's bag and in Gmail (with notes addressed to her, to me, to her mother, and anyone else I could think of). My goal was to have these notes available to me wherever I was. And yet I still found myself unable to remember at times which drug was which.

I made sure everyone involved in Jeanne's care had all her doctors' complete names and contact information. Sharing information with others becomes particularly critical during a crisis. It's lucky that there are so many tools today that make it easy and cheap to do this. For example, there are Web sites where you can set up a group call list. If you need to spread urgent information to multiple people, you dial one number and leave one voicemail. As soon as you hang up, everyone in your group call list gets a phone call. When they answer, they hear your message (and if they don't answer, your message goes into their voicemail). Of course, you can use these services in your everyday business, to inform your sales staff out in the field that a meeting has just been canceled, for example. But more importantly, you could use them in extraordinary circumstances, like to quickly provide your siblings with urgent updates about your ailing parent's health status. (See the "Stuff We Love" appendix for some suggested communications tools.) In fact, many of the tools and strategies I outline in this book are incredibly handy in a crisis—which is all the more reason to have them in place *before* the unexpected happens.

The Capacity for Now

When faced with an extremely difficult situation, I try to think ahead. But as we all know, we can't predict the future. We can only try to recognize the signposts that something bad is happening or may be about to happen and then try to be as prepared as we can so that when things start spiraling out of control, we'll have some course of action in mind.

But you can overdo it. When we plan too much in advance, trying to foresee every crisis that *might* be on the horizon, we tax those mental resources we need to get through the present moment. In other words, when we think too much about what's next, we often lose the moment we're in. I know that sounds New Agey. But, oh, how true it is, at least for me.

While Jeanne was ill, I wanted to be ready for that awful moment we knew was coming. I wanted to be at peace when it arrived. And all that time I spent mentally preparing myself, thinking ahead, was ultimately a waste of time. I was a wreck anyway when she died. Worse than that, I wasted time I could have spent just being with Jeanne, rather than preparing to be without her.

Ultimately, being organized means that when a crisis occurs, you still have the capacity for now—the ability to be in the moment. When you can do that, you don't waste time and mental energy trying to predict or ready yourself for the future, which you'll never fully be able to do. It's counterproductive to work yourself up and stress yourself out over what might happen next—because really, it could be anything.

Developing a capacity to live in the now is something that takes practice. I'm still working on it, as you'll see in the epilogue. But because of Jeanne's death, I take more pictures than I used to. I try new things even when I think I might not like them. I'm more appreciative of the gifts I've been given in life, the luck I've had.

And when I need to get out of my head and be in the moment, I ride my motorcycle. Yes, it can be scary. And, as with anything else in life, there's always the risk of a collision. But riding my motorcycle puts me *in* the world.

Picture, as I often do, a late summer afternoon. I'm riding to a motorcycle rally in Hollister, California. On the last leg of the trip, I turn down a road that twists its way through fields of strawberries. It's nearly harvest time. The fields are ablaze in red and the air is sweet with their scent.

> Felt so good to me / Finally feelin' free.
>
> —Bob Seger, "Roll Me Away"

I'm cruising on my motorcycle, the sun's on my face, life is good.

ENCODE THIS

- When you're faced with huge, unexpected challenges, everything in your world gets tested. It's even more difficult to make reasonable, unemotional decisions. You can't concentrate. You forget things because you're stressed; you're stressed because you forget things. In AA language, you hit bottom.

- Accept the fact you'll make mistakes during stressful times. The mistakes will feel even bigger than they would under everyday circumstances. Don't beat yourself up over them. Organize around this constraint as much as possible—especially with a little help from your friends, coworkers, or anyone else you trust.

- During difficult times, it's even more important to have others around you who are different from you. You'll need them to be strong when you're not, to think clearly when you can't. It's okay; that's what friends do for each other.

- When you're facing a huge challenge, a typical response is to seek more information. Unfortunately, you may soon feel flooded by all the information you're getting, particularly if it's conflicting or it's outside your areas of knowledge. Use the tools you've developed to organize your information as much as possible. Filter, take lots of notes, and share your notes online with anyone who might benefit.

- You can't predict the future. But you can identify the signposts that indicate something bad is happening. And you can try to have a plan for how you'll deal with that situation if it occurs.

- But try to "be in the moment" anyway. If you've gotten yourself organized *before* the crisis occurs, you'll have more mental energy, more space, for the here and now.

chapter 15

PUTTING IT ALL TOGETHER

I N THIS BOOK, I'VE offered twenty-one principles of organi-zation (which I'll recount at the end of this chapter). Some may make perfect sense for you; others, not so much. Whatever the case, I'd like to encourage you now to try applying at least a few of these principles to your life, to see which ones are best suited for the challenges you might currently be facing.

To give one example of how you might do this, let's consider a challenge all of us face at some point in our working lives: finding a job. This is a big deal because the stakes are high, and the entire process can be extremely stressful and overwhelming. Of course, finding a job involves effective networking, writing a killer résumé, and putting your best self forward in interviews. Ultimately, though, it's also about being well organized—and managing a lot of information. So here are ways you could apply some principles of this book to the task of finding a new job.

Principle no. 4: Use stories to remember. In a job interview, you're going to be expected to sound knowledgeable about the company you hope to work for. This will require some encoding. So when trying to remember key facts about the company, or the industry it's in, try to weave them into a story. Also, it helps to tell the people interviewing you for a job a few carefully chosen stories (by "stories" I mean anecdotes, not tall tales)—in particular, ones that show what you've success-fully accomplished at other jobs. After all, they're probably talking to a lot of other candidates, and your stories will help *them* remember *you*.

Principle no. 5: Just because something's always been done a certain way doesn't mean it *should* be. Translation: Think creatively about the problems facing the company you want to work for. If you can offer them a fresh perspective in a constructive way, you're bound to show your value and improve your chances of landing the job.

Principle no. 7: Organize around actual constraints, not assumed ones. Do you lack the experience, skill, or education that's a stated requirement for a particular job? If so, is this an actual constraint for you? Or is it something you can change? (Keep in mind some job listings overstate the necessary qualifications, in hopes of discouraging vast numbers of people from applying.) Identifying your actual constraints before applying for a job can help you stay focused, avoid wasting time, and minimize disappointment, though I'd also hasten to remind you of principle no. 9, which is, Know when to ignore your constraints, not to mention principle no. 11, Be flexible about how you achieve your goals.

Principle no. 15: Dedicate time each week to reviewing key information. In terms of looking for a job, this could mean setting aside an hour every day to read online job postings, reviewing your notes about the interviews you've had so far and the people you've contacted, and rereading the Web pages you've bookmarked about particular companies. This also brings to mind principle no. 14, Break big chunks into small ones. A job search is a huge project, one that is usually best tackled one step at a time.

Principle no. 17: Whenever possible, use the tools you already know. How are you going to track all the information you'll accumulate during your job search, such as which companies you've applied to; whom you've contacted and when; what the response was to your initial inquiry; and what the next steps are. You could buy a database application or find a project management tool online. But adding a new tool requires at least some learning curve, not to mention that it can add expense. I'd start by using a tool you're already familiar with to gather all this information, such as a Google Docs spreadsheet. In the spreadsheet, you could track and visually display in an orderly, row-and-column format, all your job search notes. And because it's a Google Docs spreadsheet, you could add to it or read it wherever you are. Alternatively, you could set up a Microsoft Excel spreadsheet and sync it to your Windows Mobile or other smart phone (though I'm not a big fan of synchronizing, in general). Bottom line: When faced with a big challenge like finding a job, try the tools you already know how to use first. If they don't serve your goals, find something that will.

Principle no. 18: Add relevant keywords to your digital information so you can easily find it later. In this case, I'd amend this principle slightly to say, *Add relevant keywords to your digital information so potential employers can easily find you.* Search is essential to so many things we do today—and it's particularly important in getting a job. Most companies use software tools designed to filter out the majority of résumés they receive. If your résumé doesn't contain certain keywords, if won't make its way to human eyes (unless you know someone at the company, of course). That's why it's so important to pay careful attention to the keywords that are sprinkled throughout a job posting and then to include the most relevant ones in your résumé and cover letter.

Granted, not all my principles of organization will apply to every challenge you face. But I'll bet at least some of them will be relevant to certain challenges at certain times. It is my hope that this book has helped you to figure out how you might apply these organizational principles—or variations of them—to each new situation you face, as you face it.

PRINCIPLES OF ORGANIZATION—A RECAP

1. Organize your life to minimize brain strain.

2. Get stuff out of your head as quickly as possible.

3. Multitasking can actually make you less efficient.

4. Use stories to remember.

5. Just because something's always been done a certain way doesn't mean it *should* be.

6. Knowledge is not power. The *sharing* of knowledge is power.

7. Organize around actual constraints, not assumed ones.

8. Be completely honest—but never judgmental—with yourself.

9. Know when to ignore your constraints.

10. Know exactly where you're going—and how you'll get there—before you start the engine.

11. Be flexible about how you achieve your goals.

12. Don't organize your information; search for it.

13. Only keep in your head what truly needs to be there.

14. Break big chunks into small ones.

15. Dedicate time each week to reviewing key information.

16. There's no such thing as a perfect system of organization.

17. Whenever possible, use the tools you already know.

18. Add relevant keywords to your digital information so you can easily find it later.

19. Take notes to help you shift contexts later.

20. Group tasks with similar contexts together.

21. Integrate work with life instead of trying to balance the two.

DUDE! JUST TURN OFF YOUR BRAIN AND SKI

SO, **DEAR READER, WE'VE** come to the end of our time together. We started this journey with a story about my childhood. As you probably gathered, that tale wasn't really about learning to do math; it was about the fact that each of us is different and must approach organization (and life) in our own unique ways. Some of the tips I've given throughout this book will work for you; others will be totally wrong. That's okay. The point was to get you thinking about what's right, and what's wrong, for you, and give you the strategies, the tools, and knowledge you need to construct your own system—one that works best for your brain, your personality, and your life.

> Just a song before I go / To whom it may concern.
>
> —Crosby, Stills & Nash, "Just a Song Before I Go"

In today's fast-paced, information-saturated world, we struggle to keep our heads above water. We use incredible amounts of mental energy to handle all the information, all the tasks, and all the challenges, that confront us every day. Then, when the unexpected happens, we have nothing left in our reserves. Why not? As you've undoubtedly figured out by now, you can thank that three-pound marvel between your ears. Your brain is incredibly powerful, but it isn't opti-mized to handle a world with so many contexts and so much

Dude! Just Turn off Your Brain and Ski

218

information overload. Remember, your brain is really good at noticing some things, but it's often prone to errors. And it has a limited capacity for attending to, much less remembering, all the countless bits of information we try, albeit unsuccessfully, to keep in our heads.

If those challenges weren't enough, the world outside your ears is terrible for you. It's organized to solve problems you no longer have or should no longer have. So we end up sacrificing our personal and family lives to work harder and harder for gains in productivity that often don't come because, yes, we're working harder, but we're not always working smarter. And then we feel unfulfilled and stressed by the day's end. This stress makes us struggle even more to get our day-to-day tasks checked off. The struggle, of course, makes us more stressed. Lo and behold, the dreaded downward spiral rears its ugly head.

How do we break out of that spiral? Well, it would help if we could reengineer our brains to have unlimited capacity for storing and processing information. Or if we could replace our societal structures and norms to match the way we really think, live, and work. But neither of these things is likely to happen in the near future. So it's more important than ever that we learn how to build our own tools, structures, and techniques to keep ourselves as organized and stress-free as possible in a disorganized, stressful world.

> **No one can find the rewind button.**
>
> —Anna Nalick,
> "Breathe (2 AM)"

Here's one final story to show you why it's so important to get things out of our heads, so we can focus all our brainpower where it's really needed.

A few years ago, I went on a skiing trip with a close friend. At that time, I was still learning the sport but had decided I was competent enough to venture onto some difficult terrain. Soon I found myself poised at the top of a particularly steep slope, and I was...deeply intimidated. Standing atop those two strangely shaped sticks attached to my feet, I wasn't sure how I could make it down the mountain without losing a limb.

I studied the slope before me, carefully, like a jeweler eyeballing a diamond ring. I tried to make out every bump and crevice from the top of the slope to the bottom. I tried to memorize each and every possible turn, to visualize my trip down the mountain—when I'd shift my weight, when I'd pick up speed, when I might fall flat on my face if I weren't supercareful.

But with each mental calculation, I was growing less and less confident about the run. In fact, I was growing downright reluctant. As I stood there, frozen in place, my buddy—a terrific skier and an even better friend—slid up next to me with ease. He looked me over, sized me up.

"Dude!" he said with a grin. "Just turn off your brain and ski!"

Having shared that piece of Zen wisdom, he did a quick hop-turn onto the slope and breezed downhill without, as far as I could tell, any forethought whatsoever.

So I tried it. I took a deep breath, aimed my skis downhill, and shoved off. I didn't think. I just rode the skis, letting my knees pick up the bumps, keeping my weight forward down the hill, turning to keep myself in control, and yet, at the same time, giving up "control."

It was one of the best runs I've ever had.

Afterward, I realized I couldn't have foreseen all the bumps or planned out and memorized all the turns I should take. My brain couldn't have assessed the precise snow conditions or predict the trajectories of other skiers on the run (and whether theirs would unexpectedly collide with my own). I realized that the reason the run had been so exhilarating was because I had simply kept my skis apart, leaned forward, relaxed my legs, and stopped thinking so hard.

I look back on that experience often. None of us can foresee all the bumps before we hit them. We can't move the trees, we can't change the gradation of a hill. We can only propel ourselves forward and trust that we'll make it to the bottom of the mountain unharmed, exhilarated, and, in every sense, alive.

Throughout this book, I've stated that a big benefit of organizing your life is to make yourself more effective, more productive, and less stressed. To stop getting in your own way. To prepare yourself for crises and challenges when they come.

You think this story's over / But it's ready to begin.

—Beastie Boys, "Paul Revere"

That's all true. But even more importantly, organizing your life frees you up to fully experience your life. Yes, it takes work to be organized, and to stay organized. But the reward is well worth the effort, I promise.

Okay, are you ready? Are your skis waxed and your knees bent? Are you leaning forward? Great. Now take a deep breath, turn off your brain, and ski.

I'll see you on the lift.

STUFF WE LOVE

THROUGHOUT THIS BOOK, I've talked about the products and services I use to be better organized. Many of them are from Google. I'm partial to Google products not because I worked there but because they fit my philosophy of what we need from our tools today. We need to store our important information in the cloud, so it's the same no matter which computer or device we use to access it. We need our tools to be easy to use and to give us tons of storage space (so we don't have to delete information). And we need the flexibility to store, search, filter, and share our information in the way that makes the most sense for us. Google tools, in general, do the best job of accomplishing these (and other) goals.

What follows is an opinionated guide to the tools I personally love, plus some alternatives that I like, and some I dislike. (As I've said, organization isn't one size fits all, so what works for me won't work for everyone, and vice versa.) I've also included input from my coauthor, Jim, and some of my most tech-savvy friends and colleagues. Since technology, like time, is always slippin' into the future, some—maybe all—of these tools may have been altered, expanded, or otherwise updated by the time you read this. Even so, the reasons why I recommend (or don't recommend) them most likely won't have changed.

And just for the fun of it, this guide concludes with music. I've pulled together some of the playlists I listened to, or was motivated by, while writing this book. Will these songs help you be better organized? Not a chance. But I hope they'll inspire you, move you, or just cause you to roll your car windows down on a sunny day and sing along, loudly.

Search Engines

LOVE

Google (google.com) is so widely used because it has an uncluttered interface, it's fast, and because its engine uses the best algorithms, so you'll usually find what you're looking for on the first page or two of results. The Google toolbar, which replaces the search window right in your browser, lets you conveniently run a Google search from any page on the Web. Google searches are also very good at helping you find images, maps, definitions, and pretty much any other piece of information under the sun.

LIKE

Yahoo! (yahoo.com) is another popular search engine. The Yahoo! home page is way too busy, but you can focus just on search at search.yahoo.com.

Kosmix.com (kosmix.com) organizes search results into categories, such as videos, news, and photos.

Bing (bing.com) is a huge improvement over Microsoft's previous search tool, Windows Live Search. It's especially useful for researching and planning travel. Overall, the quality of search results isn't as good as Google, however. By the way, you can compare Google and Bing results side-by-side at bing-vs-google.com.

DISLIKE

Ask.com (ask.com) started life as Ask Jeeves. This engine lets you search by asking a question in plain language, such as "How do clouds form?" (There's also a version for kids at AskKids.com.) This is a good idea, but the engine isn't very good at interpreting the question, so it doesn't always have great search results.

Desktop Search

LOVE

Quicksilver (quicksilver.en.softonic.com/mac) is hugely popular with productivity geeks. It's a desktop search tool for Macs, but it's also a powerful application management and/or launcher tool. Example: You can use Quicksilver to launch your Mail application and begin an e-mail to someone, all in just a few keystrokes. Quicksilver requires a bit of setup, but it's extremely helpful.

LIKE

Google Desktop (desktop.google.com) is a free download that uses Google technology to search the contents of your computer's hard drives. It works with Windows, Mac, and Linux machines, and it searches all types of files. However, the indexing process can be slow, and it consumes a lot of the computer's power. In fact, I often turn it off to save computer resources.

The Mac and Windows operating systems each have their own search tools that come built into the operating system, and they're okay. Start with them, and if they don't do the trick, try Google Desktop. (In Windows Vista, you can start a search by launching the Start menu and typing your query into the Start Search field at the bottom of the menu. To start a search on a Mac, click the magnifying glass icon that's always on the upper right corner of the screen.)

E-mail

LOVE

Gmail (mail.google.com) is a nearly ideal scaffold. It lets you store and retrieve your information from one central place. You can label and filter e-mails automatically. And it uses Google search, which means you can find stuff easily. Gmail gives you a huge amount of storage for free, so you'll probably never have to delete any messages, and it organizes e-mails in threads, so you can keep track of conversations. Gmail's spam fighting technology is terrific, which is worth noting—you'll get far fewer e-mails trying to convince you to buy pharmaceuticals! Gmail can be your communications hub, giving you instant messaging, text messaging, and video chat in addition to e-mail. You can easily consolidate multiple e-mail accounts into one Gmail account. And an off-line feature allows you to read your messages without a network connection.

LIKE

Zoho Mail (mail.zoho.com) is part of the Zoho suite of cloud productivity and collaboration services that all work together (you can see them all at zoho.com). As of this writing, Zoho Mail doesn't offer all the features I love about Gmail, such as the ability to have video chats. But, like Gmail, it offers an off-line mode (using Google technology), so you can access your messages without an Internet connection. It has no storage limits or ads; you can organize your messages with labels (as you can with Gmail) or with folders, or both. And you can view messages either as threaded conversations or in the more conventional, one-message-at-a-time manner. The site is also optimized for use on iPhones, BlackBerrys, and other mobile phones.

DISLIKE

Windows Live Hotmail (mail.live.com) is popular, especially among those used to Microsoft Outlook who migrated to a cloud e-mail service. If that's what you're looking for, give it a try. But I don't see much to recommend it. For starters, Microsoft actually discourages you from using too much storage, too soon. If your inbox gets too full, Windows Live Hotmail may send you an e-mail asking you to move e-mails from Windows Live Hotmail to your desktop, or delete some old e-mails. Windows Live Hotmail also displays annoyingly large, busy, cheeseball ads next to your messages (compared to the less obtrusive text ads you see in Gmail), among other deficiencies.

Yahoo! Mail (mail.yahoo.com) and AOL Mail (mail.aol.com) are also popular cloud e-mail services. Both offer unlimited e-mail storage. But like Windows Live Hotmail, I dislike them because they subject you to some annoying display ads.

Outlook (office.microsoft.com) I don't like Outlook for several reasons. The most important is that it is often used in conjunction with Microsoft Exchange. Exchange e-mail systems generally work well in a server environment. But because e-mail servers are expensive, users often don't have enough storage space to keep years of messages. Also, remote access to e-mail in an Exchange e-mail system can be more difficult than accessing e-mail from a cloud service like Gmail. Plus, Outlook 2007 has a clumsy system for filing e-mails. You can't give e-mails multiple labels or file them in more than one place, which makes them difficult to find later.

That said, there are lots of utilities you can add to Microsoft Outlook to help you better organize your e-mail. Here are two plug-ins I know of but don't have any opinions about:

ClearContext (clearcontext.com) automatically prioritizes messages in Outlook by looking at whom you reply to most often. Then it color-codes your messages to help you quickly figure out which ones are most important.

Xobni (xobni.com) gives you more information about people you correspond with, displayed in a sidebar within Outlook. Click on a message and Xobni will show you that person's phone number (if it's listed in your Outlook contacts), how often you correspond with that person, your most recent conversations, and so on.

You can find other add-ons by Googling terms like *outlook plug-ins, outlook add-ons, outlook utilities,* or *outlook add-ins.*

Other Communication Tools

LOVE

Adium (adiumx.com) is a free, downloadable Mac tool that allows you to access multiple instant messaging services in one place. You can also change the appearance of the interface, which I love. Currently, my Adium is configured to look like a purple cartoon bird (gotta love the purple). And in case you aren't a Mac user, Adium also has a free sibling program for Windows PCs called Pidgin, www.pidgin.im.

LIKE

Google Voice (google.com/voice) Like Gmail, Google Voice is a game changer. It gives you a lot of sophisticated phone features right on your computer or mobile device for free, including one number that rings simultaneously on multiple phones, voicemail-to-e-mail transcription, conference calling, and call recording. Although it has limitations, Google Voice is on a path toward becoming a really great communications tool.

Skype (skype.com) combines good-quality video chats, instant messaging, and free Voice over IP calls to other Skypers. It's easy to use, and with the SkypeOut service, you can call landline and cell phones for extremely low rates. There are versions of Skype for the iPhone, Windows Mobile, and other mobile operating systems too.

Twitter (twitter.com) isn't a productivity or organizational tool per se. It's a microblogging service, which means it lets you write up to 140 characters about anything and blast it to your followers. People can receive your tweets on their phones, on their computers, or even as updates to your Facebook page. You can also search previous or even real-time tweets—it's a good way to see what people are saying about a given topic. I use Twitter as an activity trace. I update frequently with a brief sentence of what I'm doing or what I just observed. I use Tweetie on my iPhone (atebits.com/tweetie-iphone) to send Twitter updates. But there are loads of other tweeting tools for mobile phones and computers, such as the Twitter Toolbar (thetwitter-toolbar.com), which lets you post and follow tweets from any browser page in Mozilla Firefox and Microsoft Internet Explorer. And Ping.fm (ping.fm) is a free service that lets you simultaneously update Twitter, Facebook, LinkedIn, and lots of other social networks.

Phonevite (phonevite.com) My coauthor, Jim, recommends this tool as an easy way to send a voicemail to multiple people at once. After setting up an account and a group contact list, you dial one number and leave a message. Within seconds, your message is sent automatically to every phone number in a specified group. Leaving the same voicemail simultaneously for multiple people makes it easy to quickly spread urgent information.

Online Backup, Storage, and File Syncing

LOVE

Dropbox (getdropbox.com) is a terrific, shared "disk" that lives in the cloud. You can use it to store information you want to make public (that is, to share with others) or keep private. I use it to store and back up files, like this chapter, that I may want to access and edit from various computers. It's also great for storing or sharing large files with coworkers, especially if your company's e-mail system puts limits on attachment sizes. I use this feature all the time.

Windows Live Sync (sync.live.com) Yes, there are Microsoft products that get some love—particularly Windows Live Sync. Jim recommends this as a free tool for syncing designated folders between multiple Macs and Windows computers. Using this service, if you make a change to a file on your Mac, within seconds, the same file on your Windows computer gets updated. If you use multiple computers on a regular basis, Windows Live Sync will simplify your life. The downside: As I've mentioned, synchronizations can be fragile, but Windows Live Sync does a pretty good job of preventing confusion caused by version conflicts.

LIKE

Google Sync (google.com/mobile/products/sync.html) lets you sync your contacts and calendar appointments on your iPhone, BlackBerry, or other phones with your Google account. It's free, and it works so well, you might not even need a service like Apple's MobileMe.

MobileMe (apple.com/mobileme) is Apple's cloud service for syncing e-mail, contacts, and calendars between Macs, Windows, iPhones, and iPod Touch players. You can also use it to store and share photos and files. It does well at some of these tasks (Sonya and I use it to sync our address books between various machines), and a so-so job at others (I much prefer Google Calendars to MobileMe's calendar).

Mozy (mozy.com) Jim uses Mozy for online backup. Mozy works with Windows and Mac computers. For a low annual fee, you can back up all the files on your hard drive to the cloud. Should you need to retrieve them later, you can go online and download them. Or for an additional fee, you can have Mozy send you all your backed-up files on DVD.

SugarSync (sugarsync.com) syncs files between multiple Macs and Windows computers and acts as an online backup/remote access service. There are versions for Windows Mobile, the iPhone, and BlackBerrys too. It offers more features than Mozy.com, but it is also more expensive.

DISLIKE

Synchronizations in general Syncing, even with great devices with good synchronization services, is a fragile process prone to errors, and it often breaks in confusing ways. Unfortunately, we're stuck with it until there is ubiquitous network access, and we can keep absolutely all of our data in one place (the cloud).

To-Do List Managers and Productivity Tools

LOVE

Things (culturedcode.com/things) is an excellent tool for organizing tasks and to-do lists. You can add tags for easier searching, assign areas of responsibility to tasks, and view all your outstanding tasks in a daily agenda. It syncs with iCal on the Mac and the iPhone Things app. Other than Gmail and Twitter, Things is probably the application I use the most.

LIKE

Remember the Milk (rememberthemilk.com) is a fairly basic to-do list originally developed, as you may have guessed, to make shopping lists. It's a Web-based tool, which you can access using software on iPhones, BlackBerrys, and other devices. This isn't my to-do list application of choice, but my friend Alex uses it all the time.

Gmail Tasks is an extremely simple to-do list manager, but it might be all you need. It lets you create a task from an e-mail with one click. You can maintain multiple lists of tasks and assign a date to each task too. Deadline-driven to-dos will also show up as a list displayed in Google Calendar (to view them, click "Tasks" in the upper-left corner of the GCal browser window). GCal also creates a separate

GCal calendar called "Tasks" automatically. But Gmail Tasks offers few of the organizational features of Things and other dedicated to-do list applications.

Jott (jott.com) Jim recommends this as a useful productivity tool for when you're on the go. If you dial Jott's toll-free number and leave yourself a quick message or reminder, the service will transcribe your message into text and e-mail it to you, within a few minutes. You can even integrate your "jotts" with Google Calendar or Microsoft Outlook, to create new appointments and reminder alerts just by talking into your phone. There's a voicemail-to-text transcription feature and an iPhone application too.

Web Browsers and Plug-ins

LOVE

Mozilla Firefox (mozilla.com/firefox) gets kudos for lots of reasons. Firefox makes bookmarks easy to search, organize, and annotate. The browser is fast and secure, there are tons of useful plug-ins, and it's available for Macs, Windows, and Linux computers.

Xmarks (xmarks.com) Speaking of useful browser plug-ins, this one is at the top of the list. It stores a version of your Firefox bookmarks in the cloud and automatically syncs them across multiple Mac and Windows machines so you can access them from anywhere. Xmarks (formerly Foxmarks) works with the Microsoft Internet Explorer and Apple Safari browsers too.

LIKE

Google Chrome (google.com/chrome) is relatively new, as browsers go (it debuted after Internet Explorer, Firefox, and Safari). The interface takes some getting used to.

Greasemonkey (greasespot.net) is a free plug-in available for a variety of browsers (the URL here is for the Firefox version, the one I use). Greasemonkey is a scripting language that allows you to customize Web pages using JavaScript. It's commonly used to change the way a particular Web page looks or to add features to the page. For example: Using a Greasemonkey script, you could easily play MP3 files you found in a Google search right there in your Google results page, without having to go to a different page or download an MP3 file. To get the maximum benefit, Greasemonkey requires a bit of scripting, which is a barrier to many people. But there are thousands of free Greasemonkey scripts available for downloading, and the tool is useful if you're willing to learn.

RSS Readers

LOVE

None. I don't love any of the RSS readers because none yet has the organizational tools I want: a terrific user interface and a supereasy way to personalize my feeds. I read blogs to learn more about a topic, or make myself laugh, or read opinions that I disagree with. I want to be able to read posts on a topic I care about, regardless of who wrote the post. Although one can do this using a combination of blog search and other tools, it isn't simple to do.

LIKE

Google Reader (google.com/reader) I receive most of my news, blog updates, and other Web content as RSS feeds, rather than going to the Web sites that produce the content. Google Reader allows me to see what's new without having to dig through multiple sites or, even worse, miss something that interests me. Google Reader, an RSS feed manager, is very good at this. I use it daily. It allows you to share articles with friends, and it offers a quick skim feature. I'm not crazy about the user interface, but I can live with it.

Sharing Documents in the Cloud

LOVE

No winners here either. I want rich tools to track changes across different editors, an easy-to-use interface, and richer features. Hmm, this is probably a good start-up company idea for someone!

LIKE

Google Docs (docs.google.com) is missing a lot of the features you'd get with Microsoft Office applications like the ability to track changes. But the suite of cloud software applications (text, spreadsheet, presentations, and forms) is useful for basic, real-time document collaboration.

There are other options, such as **GoToMeeting (gotomeeting. com) and WebEx (webex.com)**. They're fine for small businesses hosting Web meetings, in which participants view a common desktop. Such services let you see a list of who the other participants are, send an instant message to the rest of the group, and so on. But when you want to collaborate on content creation, Google Docs is fast and simple, and it's probably all you'll need.

Calendars

LOVE

Google Calendar (google.com/calendar) works for me because it makes it easy to share my calendars with others, it syncs directly with the calendar on my iPhone, and I can search it using Google tools. My personal favorite feature is that you can get reminders via SMS. Since I always have my phone with me, no matter where I am, I can find out what I'm late for.

LIKE

CalenGoo (calengoo.dgunia.de) is an iPhone app that works with Google Calendar and provides a few features, such as a weekly calendar view, that Google Calendar doesn't currently doesn't offer on iPhones. The downside: Unlike Google Calendar, CalenGoo is not a free app, though it's just a few dollars.

DISLIKE

Outlook (office.microsoft.com) is simply the wrong model for what we need in our calendars, given how we live and work today. For one thing, Outlook won't let you share your calendar with people outside your company, which forces a division between work and life. How does that help you be better organized?

E-book Readers

LOVE

Amazon Kindle (amazon.com/kindle) I love having the ability to carry a bunch of books on vacation all in one gadget. I can buy a book from the Kindle store and have it downloaded directly to the device within seconds. I can also subscribe to Kindle versions of major periodicals, such as the *New York Times, Wall Street Journal,* and *Newsweek.* I guarantee that wherever you see me, I'm carrying my Kindle. And I've probably got it open to some dumb science-fiction novel.

DISLIKE

Sony e-book reader (sonystyle.com) I so wanted to like the Sony e-book reader. It has a great physical layout; it's the perfect shape to fit into my bags. The reader itself is truly lovely, as you'd expect from one of the greatest gadget companies in the world. However, the software you have to use to find books and load them onto the device is horrendous; the search features are awful; and the software runs only on PCs. As you can imagine, none of this worked for me. So my Sony reader sits in some box, somewhere in my office.

Laptops

LOVE

Apple MacBook Air (apple.com/macbookair) It's missing some features other laptops have, like a built-in DVD drive, and it's pricey. But I can deal with all that because this is one sleek, ultralight, gorgeous laptop. It is, of course, a full-featured Mac OS computer that's powerful enough to run most common software. But it weighs only three pounds—about the same as our brains weigh, come to think of it. I love mine both because it's light enough to carry everywhere *and* because it's a piece of art. You can figure out which MacBook Air is mine by the stickers on it. At the moment, I have a Reaperwear sticker and another that says "Can't sleep, clowns will eat me." (I'm sure there's some bit of my warped psychology there, but I don't know what it is.)

LIKE

Lenovo X series tablet PCs (shop.lenovo.com) are great traveling machines if you use Windows. They're light and have decent battery lives, and there are docking stations available if you have a regular place to settle down with it. This is the only Windows machine I use.

Tools for Organizing Your Health Information

LOVE

Google Health (google.com/health) As you can imagine, given Jeanne's story, I've been waiting impatiently for a tool that helps people organize important health care information. Google Health is what I've been waiting for. First, it gives you a simple way to enter and update current health care status. Plus, it helps you keep track of all your past medical activity including dates of last checkups; names of medications you've taken (and any reactions you might have had to them); names and phone numbers of doctors you've seen; and lists of any surgeries, tests, vaccines, treatments or procedures you've undergone or received, and when. Since the information is stored in the cloud, you can get to it from anywhere; there's no need to carry loads of copies around with you to make sure you have the data. It also integrates with several online pharmacies to manage your drug lists and availability. I wish I'd had these tools when Jeanne was ill.

Mood Music

As you've undoubtedly noticed, I'm a music fanatic. As I was writing just about every word in this book, there was background music playing.

So to conclude our journey together, I put together a few playlists of music I love. These songs—not to mention the performers, songwriters, and lyricists who made them possible—have helped me through this book and through many parts of my life. I'm indebted to them all.

Here, then, is some aural art. I hope you enjoy it. And if you download any of these songs, please do it legally and pay for them. Thank you!

SONGS TO RELAX BY

1. Anna Nalick, "Breathe (2 AM)"
2. Guns N' Roses, "Patience"
3. Alannah Myles, "Black Velvet"
4. Nanci Griffith, "I Would Bring You Ireland"
5. Neil Young, "Thrasher"
6. Roxy Music, "Avalon"
7. Alison Krauss, "Down to the River to Pray"

SONGS TO WORK OUT YOUR STRESS TO

1. Molly Hatchet, "Flirtin' with Disaster"
2. Nirvana, "Smells Like Teen Spirit"

3. Disturbed, "Down with the Sickness"

4. Rush, "Limelight"

5. The Killers, "Spaceman"

6. Bombtrack, "Rage Against the Machine"

7. Nine Inch Nails, "Head Like a Hole"

SONGS TO CRY BY

1. Sheryl Crow, "Home"

2. Crosy, Stills & Nash, "Wasted on the Way"

3. Elton John, "Captain Fantastic and the Brown Dirt Cowboy"

4. Bob Dylan, "Boots of Spanish Leather"

5. Depeche Mode, "Precious"

6. The Smiths, "Last Night I Dreamt That Somebody Loved Me"

7. Yaz, "Mr. Blue"

SONGS TO IMAGINE YOU'RE ON VACATION BY

1. Alice Cooper, "School's Out"

2. The Alan Parsons Project, "Games People Play"

3. Sheryl Crow, "Every Day Is a Winding Road"

4. Bob Seger, "Roll Me Away"

5. R.E.M. "Driver 8"

6. The Streets, "Two Nations" (The Streets)

7. Was (Not Was), "Hello, Dad…I'm in Jail"

SONGS TO WRITE CODE BY

1. Coldplay, "Viva La Vida"

2. The Police, "Synchronicity II"

3. Incubus, "Pardon Me"

4. AC/DC, "Back in Black"

5. Arrested Development, "Tennessee"

6. My Life with the Thrill Kill Kult, "Kooler Than Jesus"

7. Smashing Pumpkins, "1979"

APPENDIX

song attributions

IN CASE YOU'RE INTERESTED, here is the complete information for all the lyrics I used in this book, along with the copyright information. All of the data come from the versions of the songs that I own, so there may be alternative data out there (from different versions of some songs).

The songs are arranged by artist, in alphabetical order. Thanks to all the copyright holders for their terrific art.

The Alan Parsons Project, "Games People Play": "Where do we go from here…And how do we spend our lives?" Copyright 2007, Sony BMG Music Entertainment, Inc. Composed by Alan Parsons and Eric Woolfson.

Beastie Boys, "Paul Revere": "You think this story's over / But it's ready to begin." Copyright 1986, Def Jam Recordings. Composed by Ad-Rock, Darryl "D.M.C." McDaniels, Rick Rubin, and Joseph Simmons.

Tracy Chapman, "Fast Car": "You got a fast car / But is it fast enough so we can fly away?" Copyright 1988, Elektra / Asylum Records. Composed by Tracy Chapman.

The Church, "Under the Milky Way": "I got no time for private consultation." Copyright 1999, Buddha Records. Composed by Karin Jansson and Steve Kilbey.

The Church, "Under the Milky Way": "Wish I knew what you were looking for." Copyright 1999, Buddha Records. Composed by Karin Jansson and Steve Kilbey.

Coldplay, "Yellow": "I drew a line for you / And it was all yellow." Copyright 2000, EMI Records. Composed by Guy Berryman, Will Champion, and Chris Martin.

Coldplay, "The Scientist": "Running in circles / Chasing our tails." Copyright 2002, EMI Records. Composed by Guy Berryman, Jon Buckland, Will Champion, and Chris Martin.

Coldplay, "Lost!": "I just got lost / Every river that I tried to cross." Copyright 2008, EMI Records. Composed by Guy Berryman, Jon Buckland, Will Champion, and Chris Martin.

Coldplay, featuring Jay-Z, "Lost+": "Is to have had and lost / Better than not having at all?" Copyright 2008, EMI Records. Composed by Guy Berryman, Jon Buckland, Will Champion, Chris Martin, and Jay-Z.

Coldplay, "Viva La Vida": "One minute I held the key / Next the walls were closed on me." Copyright 2008, EMI Records. Composed by Guy Berryman, Jon Buckland, Will Champion, and Chris Martin.

Alice Cooper, "Under My Wheels": "The telephone is ringing / You got me on the run." Copyright 2005, Warner Bros. Records. Composed by Michael Bruce, Dennis Dunaway, and Bob Ezrin.

Counting Crows, "Angels of the Silences": "Little angels of the silences / That climb into my bed and whisper." Copyright 2003, Geffen Records. Composed by Counting Crows, Adam Duritz, and Charlie Gillingham.

Crosby, Stills & Nash, "Wasted on the Way": "So much time to make up… Time we have wasted on the way." Copyright 2005, Atlantic Recording Corp. Composed by Graham Nash.

Crosby, Stills & Nash, "Just a Song Before I Go": "Just a song before I go / To whom it may concern." Copyright 2005, Atlantic Recording Corp. Composed by Graham Nash.

Sheryl Crow, "Everyday Is a Winding Road": "I've been swimming in a sea of anarchy." Copyright 2003, A&M Records. Composed by Sheryl Crow, Brian MacLeod, and Jeff Trott.

Dead Kennedys, "Take This Job and Shove It": "Take this job and shove it / I ain't working here no more." Copyright 2004, Manifesto Records. Composed by Jello Biafra and David Allan Coe.

Depeche Mode, "Precious": "Angels with silver wings / Shouldn't know suffering." Copyright 2005, Sire / Reprise. Composed by Martin L. Gore.

Disturbed, "Down with the Sickness": "Don't try to deny what you feel." Copyright 2000, Giant Records. Composed by Disturbed.

Bob Dylan, "Blowin' in the Wind": "The answer my friend / Is blowin' in the wind." Copyright 1963, Sony Music Entertainment. Composed by Bob Dylan.

Eminem, "My Name Is": "My brain's dead weight, I'm trying to get my head straight." Copyright 2005, Aftermath Entertainment/Interscope Records. Composed by Dr. Dre, Eminem.

Fine Young Cannibals, "I'm Not Satisfied": "Keep on working / till you're fit to drop." Copyright 1989, London / Sire Records. Composed by Roland Gift and David Steele.

Aretha Franklin, "Think": "Let your mind go / Let yourself be free." Copyright 1985, Atlantic Recording Corp. Composed by Aretha Franklin and Ted White.

Guns N' Roses, "Patience": "All we need is just a little patience." Copyright 2004, Geffen Records. Composed by Izzy Stradlin.

Herman's Hermits, "I'm Henry VIII, I Am": "Second verse same as the first." Copyright 2004, ABKCO Music & Records, Inc. Composed by Fred Murray and R. P. Weston.

Human League, "Human": "I'm only human/Born to make mistakes."Copyright 2005, Virgin Records. Composed by James Harris and Terry Lewis.

Incubus, "Pardon Me": "I'll never be the same."Copyright 1999, Sony Music Entertainment, Inc. Composed by Brandon Boyd, Mike Einziger, Alex Katunich, Chris Kilmore, and Jose Antonio Pasillas II.

Incubus, "Pardon Me": "Pardon me while I burst into flames." Copyright 1999, Sony Music Entertainment, Inc. Composed by Brandon Boyd, Mike Einziger, Alex Katunich, Chris Kilmore, and Jose Antonio Pasillas II.

Iron Maiden, "Still Life": "Now it's clear/And I know what I have to do." Copyright 1998, Iron Maiden Holdings Ltd. Composed by Steve Harris and David Murray.

James Gang, "Walk Away": "You just turn your pretty head and walk away." Copyright 1985, UMG Recordings, Inc. Composed by Joe Walsh.

Jefferson Airplane, "White Rabbit": "Feed your head." Copyright 2003, BMG Heritage. Composed by Grace Slick.

Elton John, "Tiny Dancer": "Looking on, she sings the songs." Copyright 1971, This Record Company Ltd. Composed by Elton John and Bernie Taupin.

K.C. & The Sunshine Band, "Get Down Tonight": "Get down tonight." Copyright 1980, T. K. Records, a label of Warner Strategic Marketing. Composed by Harry Wayne "K.C." Casey and Richard Finch.

The Killers, "Spaceman": "The spaceman says, 'Everybody look down/It's all in your mind.'" Copyright 2008, The Island Def Jam Music Group. Composed by Brandon Flowers, Dave Keuning, Mark Stoermer, and Ronnie Vannucci, Jr.

Lady Antebellum, "I Run to You": "I run my life/Or is it running me?" Copyright 2007, Capitol Records Nashville. Composed by Tom Douglas, Dave Haywood, Charles Kelley, and Hillary Scott.

Lagwagon, "The Kids Are All Wrong": "Heroes die off every day." Copyright 1998, Fat Wreck Chords. Composed by Joey Cape, Lagwagon.

Cyndi Lauper, "True Colors": "I see your true colors shining through." Copyright 1983, Sony Music Entertainment. Composed by Tom Kelly and Billy Steinberg.

Lindsay Lohan, "I Decide": "I'm gonna make my own mistakes." Copyright 2004, Walt Disney Records. Composed by D. Warren.

Molly Hatchet, "Flirtin' with Disaster": "I'm flirtin' with disaster every day." Copyright 1979, 2001 Sony BMG Music Entertainment. Composed by Danny Joe Brown, Dave Hlubek, and Banner Thomas.

Alanis Morissette, "You Learn": "Wait until the dust settles/You live, you learn." Copyright 1995, Maverick Recording Company. Composed by Glen Ballard and Alanis Morissette.

Alannah Myles, "Black Velvet": "The sun is settin' like molasses in the sky." Copyright 1989, Atlantic Recording Corporation. Composed by David Tyson and Christopher Ward.

Anna Nalick, "Breathe (2 AM)": "No one can find the rewind button." Copyright 2005, Sony BMG Music Entertainment. Composed by Anna Nalick.

Nazareth, "Love Hurts": "Love hurts." Copyright 1975, A&M Records. Composed by Boudleaux Bryant.

Nine Inch Nails, "Hurt": "I hurt myself today / To see if I still feel." Copyright 2002, TVT Records. Composed by Trent Reznor.

Nirvana, "Smells Like Teen Spirit": "Here we are now / Entertain us." Copyright 1991, Geffen Records Inc. Composed by Kurt Cobain, Dave Grohl, and Krist Novoselic.

Pink Floyd, "Mother": "Mother did it need to be so high?" Copyright 2000, Harvest / Capitol. Composed by Roger Waters.

Pink Floyd, "Time": "You run and you run to catch up with the sun / But it's sinking." Copyright 1984, Capitol. Composed by David Gilmour, Nick Mason, Roger Waters, and Rick Wright.

The Police, "Synchronicity II": "Another working day has ended / Only the rush hour hell to face." Copyright 2003, A&M Records Ltd. Composed by Sting.

Elvis Presley, "Jailhouse Rock": "Everybody in the whole cell block / Was dancin' to the jailhouse rock." Copyright 2002, BMG Music. Composed by Jerry Leiber and Mike Stoller.

The Psychedelic Furs, "Love My Way": "I follow where my mind goes." Copyright 1980, Sony Music Entertainment (UK) Ltd. Composed by John Ashton, Richard Butler, Tim Butler, and Vince Ely.

Diana Ross, Theme from *Mahogany:* "Do you know where you're going to?" Copyright 1976, Motown Records, a Division of UMG Recordings, Inc. Composed by Michael Masser and Gerald Goffin.

Bob Seger, "Roll Me Away": "Felt so good to me / Finally feelin' free." Copyright 1975, Sony Music Entertainment. Composed by Bob Seger.

Bob Seger, "Roll Me Away": "Gotta keep rollin' / Gotta keep ridin.'" Copyright 1975, Sony Music Entertainment. Composed by Bob Seger.

Paul Simon, "Kodachrome": "I got a Nikon camera / I love to take a photograph." Copyright 2007, Warner Bros. Records, a Warner Music Group company. Composed by Paul Simon.

Steely Dan, "Rikki Don't Lose That Number": "Rikki don't lose that number.... Send it off in a letter to yourself." Copyright 1985, UMG Recordings, Inc. Composed by Walter Becker and Donald Fagen.

Steely Dan, "Do It Again": "You go back, Jack / Do it again." Copyright 1972, UMG Recordings, Inc. Composed by Walter Becker and Donald Fagen.

The Steve Miller Band, "Fly Like an Eagle": "Time keeps on slippin', slippin', slippin' / Into the future." Copyright 1978, Capitol Records, Inc. Composed by Steve Miller.

Tag Team, "Whoomp! There It Is": "Whoomp! There it is." Copyright 1993, Bellmark Records. Composed by Ralph Sall, Stephen Gibson, and Cecil Glenn.

Talking Heads, "Once in a Lifetime": "Same as it ever was." Copyright 1980, Sire Records Company. Composed by David Byrne, Brian Eno, Chris Frantz, Jerry Harrison, and Tina Weymouth.

Bonnie Tyler, "Total Eclipse of the Heart": "We're living in a powder keg and giving off sparks." Copyright 2005, Soundbarrier Ltd. Composed by Jim Steinman.

Yaz (also known as Yazoo), "Nobody's Diary": "If I wait for just a second more / I know I'll forget what I came here for." Copyright 2008, Mute Records Ltd. Composed by Alison Moyet.

ACKNOWLEDGMENTS

Douglas C. Merrill:
Getting to write acknowledgments is an amazing joy—I used to read the acknowledgments in every book I read as a child, hoping that someday I'd get to write one as well. And now I get to do so, thanks to several people.

First, I need to thank my most-excellent coauthor, Jim Martin. Jim, you've been amazing through this process, bringing structure, humor, and a sense of style that made writing great fun.

Thanks go out to the Google PR team, especially Karen Wickre and the whole of the Search team, and also to Joe Kita for writing the *Men's Health* article that kicked this all off.

This work would not have been possible without the invaluable assistance of Roger and Talia, our editors. Thanks for your guidance throughout this yearlong process!

Finally, this would not have happened, and would have been far less enjoyable, without the lovely Sonya reading, commenting, joking, commiserating, and generally making me complete. Thank you.

James A. Martin:

Heartfelt gratitude to Karen Wickre for suggesting me for this project; to Douglas Merrill, for giving me the opportunity and for being an ideal collaborator; to Talia Krohn and Roger Scholl, for guiding these two novice book authors so expertly throughout the project; to Margaret Heindl and Simon Blackstein, who read drafts and offered helpful suggestions and insights; and most of all to Nick Parham, my partner, coach extraordinaire, and live-in comedian.

ENDNOTES

PREFACE

1. http://www.google.com/corporate/
2. *Wall Street Journal*, May 2, 2008, http://online.wsj.com/article/
SB120965705088459637.html

CHAPTER 1

1. http://wiki.answers.com/Q/How_much_does_a_human_
brain_weigh
2. http://en.wikipedia.org/wiki/Cocktail_party_effect
3. http://en.wikipedia.org/wiki/Waiting_for_Godot

CHAPTER 2

1. Industrial Revolution. Encyclopædia Britannica. 2008.
Encyclopædia Britannica Online. 17 June 2008 http://www.britannica
.com/eb/article-9042370
2. http://en.wikipedia.org/wiki/Eight-hour_day
3. Frederick W. Taylor. *Encyclopædia Britannica*. Retrieved January
4, 2009, from Encyclopædia Britannica Online. http://www.britannica
.com/EBchecked/topic/584820/Frederick-W-Taylor
4. http://en.wikipedia.org/wiki/Scientific_management
5. Henry Ford. *Encyclopædia Britannica*. Retrieved July 1, 2008,
from Encyclopædia Britannica Online. http://www.britannica.com/
EBchecked/topic/213223/Henry-Ford
6. http://en.wikipedia.org/wiki/Frederick_Winslow_Taylor
7. Frederick W. Taylor. *Encyclopædia Britannica*. Retrieved June 23,
2008, from Encyclopædia Britannica Online. http://www.britannica
.com/eb/article-9071464
8. http://en.wikipedia.org/wiki/
Frederick_Winslow_Taylor#Scientific_management
9. http://www.amazon.com/The-Principles-of-Scientific-
Management/dp/B0010538DU/ref=sr_1_4?ie=UTF8&s=books&qid=12310
98768&sr=8-4
10. http://www.infoplease.com/spot/schoolyear1.html
11. http://www.infoplease.com/spot/schoolyear1.html
12. http://www.psparents.net/Year_Round_School.htm
13. Karl Benz. *Encyclopædia Britannica*. Retrieved June 22, 2008,
from Encyclopædia Britannica Online. http://www.britannica.com/eb/
article-9078681

14. http://en.wikipedia.org/wiki/Interstate_highway

15. http://abcnews.go.com/Technology/Traffic/Story?id=485098&page=1

16. http://www.nytimes.com/2009/03/27/world/europe/27bus.html?_r=1

17. http://en.wikipedia.org/wiki/Journeyman

18. http://www.scribd.com/doc/6920228/NASDAQ-Ringers

CHAPTER 3

1. http://customwire.ap.org/dynamic/stories/C/CAR_NEWMANS_PASSION?SITE=WIMIL&SECTION=ENTERTAINMENT&TEMPLATE=DEFAULT&CTIME=2008-09-28-00-24-25

CHAPTER 6

1. http://www.hitwise.com/press-center/hitwiseHS2004/google-nears-searches-oct.php

2. http://en.wikipedia.org/wiki/PageRank

CHAPTER 8

1. http://www.irs.gov/businesses/small/article/0,,id=98513,00.html

2. http://www.businessweek.com/technology/content/may2008/tc20080526_547942.htm

CHAPTER 12

1. http://en.wikipedia.org/wiki/Scrum_(development)

INDEX

translations of foreign
phrases, 87
Google's initial public offering
(IPO), 35–36
Google Sync, 228
Google Voice, 226
GoToMeeting, 232
Greasemonkey, 231
Gridlock, 32
Groupthink, 101

Health information, 122,
234–235
Home office, organization of,
117–118
Home renovations, 164–165
Honesty with ourselves, 45–46,
50

Industrial Revolution, 23–24
Information storage/
organization, 107–108
democratization of
information and, 93–94
filtering and, 96–102,
105–107
goal setting and, 95–96,
111–112, 114, 116
grouping information
physically into categories,
102
importance of, 94–95
large chunks of information
broken into smaller ones,
98–99
note taking and, 101–102
reviewing of key
information, 103, 105

See also Digital information
organization; Paper-based
information organization
Instant messaging, 137
Invitation services, 157

Jet lag, 198–199
Job hunting, 213–215
Jott.com, 230

Knowledge as power, fallacy of,
33–38
Kosmix.com, 223
Krohn, Talia, 100, 101, 139, 245,
246

Labels used for filtering, 99,
138–140, 141–142
Laptops, 234
Legal documents, 116
Lenovo X series tablet PCs, 234
Long-term memory, 9, 10–12
Lugosi, Bela, 164
Lyrics appearing in this book,
xiii–xiv

Mac operating system, 223–224
Maps, access to, 87
Measurement conversions, 86
Meetings, 187–188
Memory, 3–6, 20
attention and, 8
context and, 12, 13, 16
context shifting and, 181–182

257